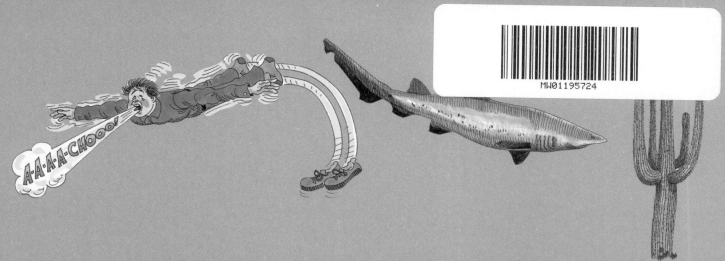

Does hay cause hay fever?•How hard does a shark bite?•**Why don't cacti have leaves?**•

How do volcanoes cause colorful sunsets?•Do woodpeckers get headaches?•Why does ice float?•

How can water break rocks?•What is the Milky Way?•**Can you find a mermaid's purse?**•

What is a food chain? • **Why don't we feel Earth's motion?** • Who was Rachel Carson? •

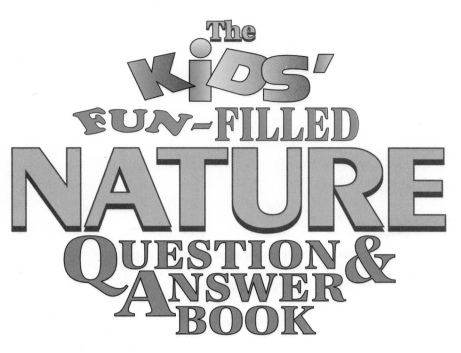

The Kids' Fun-Filled NATURE Question & Answer Book

Written by
Rebecca L. Grambo

Illustrated by
Tony Tallarico

Incorporated

Copyright © 2000 Kidsbooks, Inc., and Anthony Tallarico
3535 West Peterson Avenue
Chicago, IL 60659

Manufactured in China

Visit us at www.kidsbooks.com
Volume discounts available for group purchases.

WHAT IS A "LIVING FOSSIL"?

A plant or animal that has survived almost unchanged for millions of years. A fish called the coelacanth (SEE-luh-kanth) is a famous example. Until 1938, scientists believed that coelacanths had been extinct for 90 million years; then a living one was caught off the coast of South Africa. Sharks are also living fossils. They appeared more than 360 million years ago, long before dinosaurs.

I DIDN'T LIVE THIS LONG TO FALL FOR THAT OLD TRICK!

What are fossils?

Preserved traces of once-living things. Fossils are often bones but can also be things like teeth, wood, or shell. You can also find fossilized tracks, burrows, skin impressions, and even fossilized pieces of poop, which are called **coprolites** (KAHP-ruh-lites).

Were dinosaurs and humans ever alive at the same time?

No. Dinosaurs lived on Earth from about 245 million years ago until 65 million years ago, when most became extinct. The first known human ancestors—called *Australopithecus*—appeared about 4 million years ago. The first "modern" humans (those with bodies much like ours) did not appear until about 200,000 years ago.

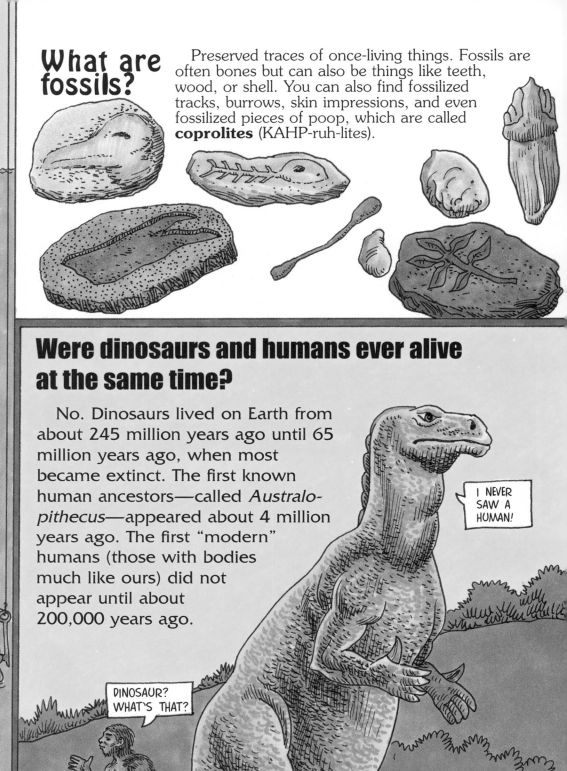

I NEVER SAW A HUMAN!

DINOSAUR? WHAT'S THAT?

Who was Charles Darwin?

Charles Darwin (1809-1882) was a naturalist (a scientist who studies the natural world). In 1859, he published *The Origin of Species*, a book that presented the theory of evolution—the idea that all plant and animal life gradually change in form, adapting to suit their environment. Darwin's ideas caused a major shift in how people view the world, and sparked debates that continue to this day.

How do we know what dinosaurs looked like?

From finding fossilized dinosaur bones and fitting them together. Scars on dinosaur bones are an important clue: They show how muscles were attached. Experts reconstruct the shape of the muscles, giving us a "picture" of what the dinosaur looked like. Skin impressions from some dinosaur fossils help scientists guess at skin texture and color, based on their knowledge of dinosaurs and living reptiles.

Pterosaurs were flying reptiles, not dinosaurs.

Do sun dogs bark?

No. Sun dogs are bright spots of light appearing on one or both sides of the sun. They are caused by sunlight passing through ice crystals in the air.

Why is the sky blue?

Molecules and dust particles in Earth's atmosphere scatter sunlight. Short light waves, such as violet and blue, scatter better than long red and orange light waves. The blue color that we see is a mix of blue, violet, green, and tiny amounts of other colors scattered across the sky. If you were standing on the moon, which does not have an atmosphere to catch and scatter light, the sky would look black.

What is a rainbow?

When sunlight shines through raindrops, it bounces off the back wall of each drop. When light exits these drops, it splits into different colors because each light wave leaves at a slightly different angle. All raindrops alter light this way. From a distance, our eyes see each color as arcs, or bows, in the sky.

What are the northern lights?

Shimmering, brightly colored bands of light that appear in the night sky near the magnetic north pole. They are caused by particles streaming from the sun, which make gases in Earth's upper atmosphere glow. The best places to see the northern lights—also called the aurora borealis—are northern Alaska, Canada's Hudson Bay, northern Norway, and northern Siberia. Southern lights—called the aurora australis—can be seen near the magnetic south pole.

Barrow, ALASKA

WOW! IT'S HUGE!

Can you see rainbows at night?

Yes. Bright moonlight shining through falling water creates an effect known as a "moonbow," which usually is much fainter than a rainbow. Cumberland Falls in Kentucky is famous for its moonbows.

9

DO FLYING FISH AND FLYING SQUIRRELS REALLY FLY?

No. They are gliders, not true fliers. Flying fish leap out of the water to escape predators, gliding for short distances on their long front fins. A flying squirrel has a thin membrane of skin that connects its front and back legs. When it leaps from a tree and spreads its limbs, the membrane acts like a parachute, helping it glide safely to the ground.

Is there such a thing as a flying fox?

Yes, but it's not a real fox. Some large bats have brown fur, pointed ears, and a foxy-looking nose. Because of these features, these bats are known as flying foxes. Flying foxes eat fruit or flower nectar and live where it is warm all year.

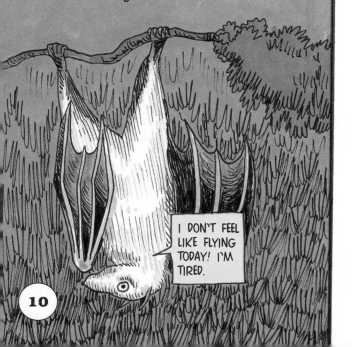

I DON'T FEEL LIKE FLYING TODAY! I'M TIRED.

What is the BIGGEST flying insect?

COMING THROUGH!

The Goliath beetle, which lives in the African rain forest, weighs 4 ounces. That's as heavy as a quarter-pound hamburger! The Goliath beetle is so strong it can peel a banana with its forelegs!

Why do birds fly in V formations?

To save energy. The first bird's wings break up the wind, and create a current on which following birds can ride. Birds take turns leading the V, or *chevron*. Scientists calculate that birds flying alone can go only about 90 percent as far as birds flying in Vs—important for birds that migrate long distances, such as geese, which travel across entire continents each spring and fall.

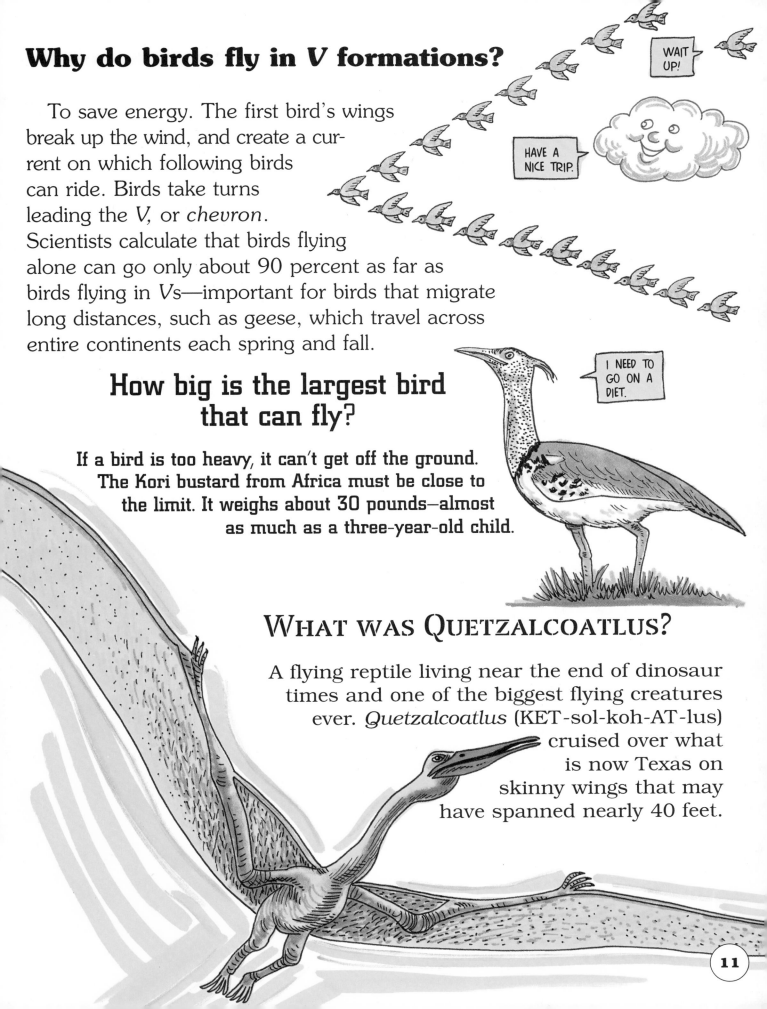

WAIT UP!

HAVE A NICE TRIP.

I NEED TO GO ON A DIET.

How big is the largest bird that can fly?

If a bird is too heavy, it can't get off the ground. The Kori bustard from Africa must be close to the limit. It weighs about 30 pounds—almost as much as a three-year-old child.

WHAT WAS QUETZALCOATLUS?

A flying reptile living near the end of dinosaur times and one of the biggest flying creatures ever. *Quetzalcoatlus* (KET-sol-koh-AT-lus) cruised over what is now Texas on skinny wings that may have spanned nearly 40 feet.

Have the continents always been where they are today?

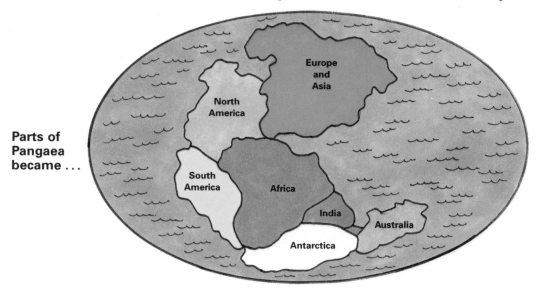

Parts of
Pangaea
became ...

Europe
and
Asia

North
America

South
America

Africa

India

Australia

Antarctica

No. They are constantly moving—very, very slowly. Sections of Earth's crust, called tectonic plates, shift over time. About 150 million years ago, all of today's continents were joined together in one supercontinent called Pangaea (pan-JEE-uh). But the sea floor spread slowly, pushing them apart. Today, Earth's eight large plates are still moving apart, at the rate of about 2 to 4 inches a year.

What causes EARTHQUAKES?

As the tectonic plates of Earth's crust move, huge stresses build up in the rocks until, finally, the rocks give way. If this happens in a series of tiny breaks, we don't feel anything, but when that stress is relieved in one big, sudden break, we have an earthquake.

Tectonic plate

Tectonic plate

Where is the Valley of Ten Thousand Smokes?

In Katmai (KAT-my) National Monument, Alaska. One of the biggest volcanic eruptions in recorded history occurred here in 1912. Visitors to the valley four years later reported steam rising from tens of thousands of "smokes," or fumaroles—holes in the valley floor near the volcano.

WHAT MADE THINGS ROCK IN NEW MADRID, MISSOURI, NEAR THE END OF 1811?

A series of earthquakes believed to be the strongest in U.S. history shook things up in that area from mid-December 1811 to March 1812. The quakes rattled two thirds of the U.S., changed the course of the Mississippi River, and created new lakes!

What is the San Andreas fault?

CALIFORNIA

Sacramento

San Francisco

San Andreas Fault

NORTH AMERICAN PLATE

PACIFIC PLATE

Los Angeles

Colorado River

San Diego

California's San Andreas fault is where two huge tectonic plates slide past each other. Hundreds of earthquakes occur here every day, most too small to be felt. During the devastating San Francisco earthquake of 1906, however, land at the San Andreas fault moved about 20 feet in a very short time! In all, there have been more than 160 major quakes in California in the last 100 years.

Why does ice float?

Substances are usually most dense when they are solid, because that is when their molecules are most compact. But water is different. Water molecules are farther apart when water is solid (ice) than when it is liquid. This means that ice is less dense than water—so it floats!

What if ice DIDN'T float?

That would be bad news for fish! Lakes and other bodies of water would freeze solid from the bottom up. We wouldn't have the same kinds of aquatic life that we do now, because aquatic animals wouldn't survive winter.

What is the temperature when it is absolutely the coldest it can get?

Absolute zero, or -459.67 degrees Fahrenheit. Scientists have been able to get within two millionths of a degree of this point in labs. Nothing moves at this temperature, not even a molecule!

What is permafrost and how can it cause problems?

Permafrost is soil that stays frozen even in summer. It is found in places close to the poles, such as Alaska and Siberia. Permafrost can cause problems for buildings constructed on it. Warmth can leak through the building's foundation, melting the permafrost, which softens the soil—making it soft enough for the building to sink!

THIS IS MY KIND OF WEATHER!

BRR ... IT'S TOO COLD HERE!

How cold does it get in Antarctica?

The lowest temperature ever recorded anywhere on Earth was -128.6 degrees Fahrenheit at Russia's Vostok research station at the South Pole, on July 21, 1983.

Why do moths circle around bright lights?

Night-flying moths navigate by staying at a constant angle to the moon. If they stick with the moon, they fly in a straight line every time. When they see artificial lights, they get confused and try navigating by them instead, but it doesn't work nearly as well! To keep the light at the same angle, the moth must keep changing direction. It ends up flying in ever-smaller circles around the light.

I'M GETTING DIZZY!

Why don't spiders get stuck in their own webs?

They avoid the sticky sections. Some spiders use dry silk for the web spokes, then lay down a circular pattern of sticky silk around it. The spider runs along the dry silk. If a leg does happen to stick, the spider uses its saliva to dissolve the glue.

What makes a firefly light up?

Other fireflies! Fireflies (also called lightning bugs) blink their lights in a code that tells what species they are, whether they are male or female, and whether they are ready to mate. The light, produced by a chemical reaction in a special organ in the firefly's abdomen, may also serve as a warning.

16

Is there really such a creature as a Tasmanian devil?

MAKE MY DAY!

Yes! The real Tasmanian devil is a marsupial (pouched mammal) about 20 to 30 inches long with a foot-long bushy tail. It has a squarish head and a stocky body. This creature's strong teeth and jaws are perfect for tearing apart meat it eats. Today, the only place you can find these little devils in the wild is Tasmania, an island that is part of Australia.

Do animals see COLOR?

Birds seem to be very good at recognizing colors. Most mammals are color-blind, but monkeys, apes, and humans can tell colors apart. Your pet dog or cat probably sees the world in black, gray, and white.

Why don't beavers get SPLINTERS in their mouths?

Mainly, because they don't chew on dry wood. They chew either live trees or water-soaked branches. Also, a beaver's lips close tightly together behind its big front teeth, which locks out bits of wood and also lets the beaver work underwater.

What is St. Elmo's fire?

Sometimes, a flamelike mass caused by electricity in the air appears at the tops of tall objects during thunderstorms. Long-ago sailors who noticed this strange light above the masts of their ships named it after their patron saint, St. Elmo. Another name for the fire is *corposant,* a name that means "holy body."

WHAT CAUSES LIGHTNING?

The rapid movement of ice crystals in storm clouds builds up electric charges (similar to the charge that builds up when you rub a balloon on your sleeve). Electric charges also form on the ground beneath the clouds. When a negative charge meets a positive charge, look out! A huge electrical current—a lightning bolt—shoots between the two charges. Most lightning stays up in the clouds; only about a quarter of it strikes the ground.

What is THUNDER?

BARROOOOM!

Lightning heats the air along its path—to temperatures as high as 54,000 degrees Fahrenheit! As it heats then cools, this air expands and contracts, forming a series of shock waves that travel at the speed of sound. Our ears pick up those fast-moving waves as the boom, crash, and rumble of thunder.

Why don't electric eels zap themselves?

For the same reason you don't get zapped by the electricity in *your* body! (Electric signals tell your muscles how to move.) Your nerves have a protective coating that shields you against your own electricity, and so do the electric eel's. But the eel's body makes far more electricity than a human's—enough to stun a horse!

HOW CAN BIRDS SIT ON POWER LINES WITHOUT GETTING ELECTROCUTED?

I FEEL GREAT!

ME, TOO!

ME THREE!

A bird sits touching only one line and nothing else through which the electricity can flow to the ground—so no current flows through its body. Trying to rescue a kite caught in electric lines is deadly dangerous, however: If a person holds onto a pole and touches a kite caught on a power line, current flows through the kite, into and through his body, then to the ground—and the human body cannot absorb such a huge shock.

How can you be moving, even when standing still?

Not only is Earth spinning on its axis at about 1,000 miles per hour, it is also zooming around the sun at more than 65,000 miles per hour. The crustal plate beneath your feet is moving, too—very, very slowly.

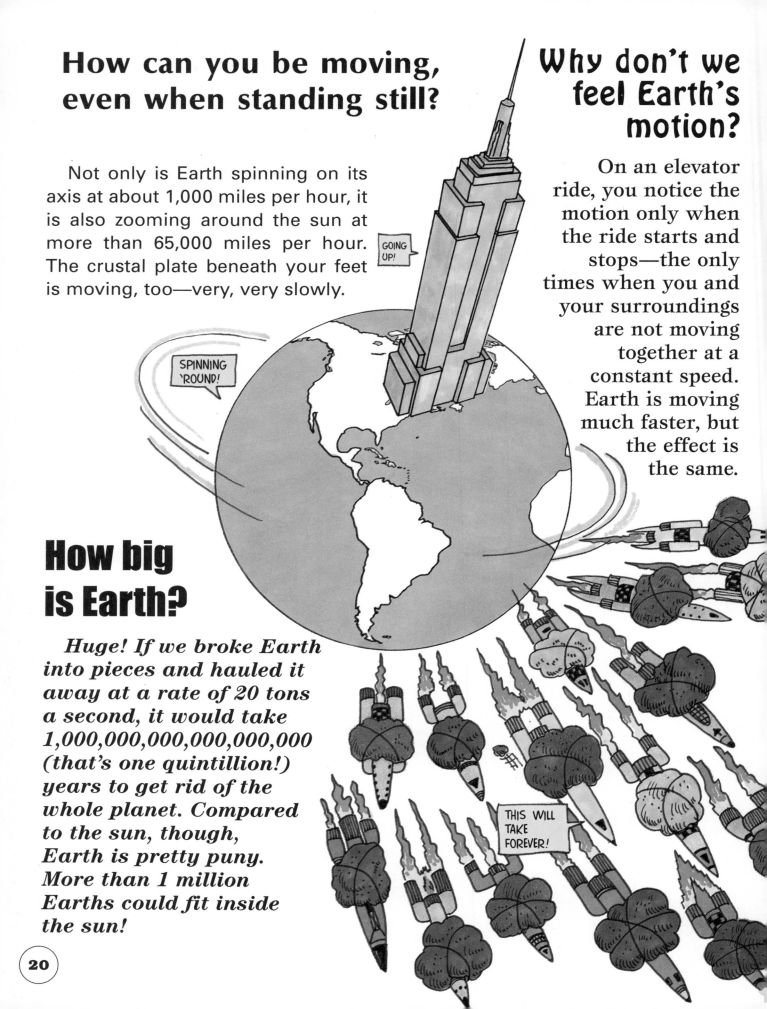

GOING UP!

SPINNING 'ROUND!

Why don't we feel Earth's motion?

On an elevator ride, you notice the motion only when the ride starts and stops—the only times when you and your surroundings are not moving together at a constant speed. Earth is moving much faster, but the effect is the same.

How big is Earth?

Huge! If we broke Earth into pieces and hauled it away at a rate of 20 tons a second, it would take 1,000,000,000,000,000,000 (that's one quintillion!) years to get rid of the whole planet. Compared to the sun, though, Earth is pretty puny. More than 1 million Earths could fit inside the sun!

THIS WILL TAKE FOREVER!

How much of Earth's surface is water?

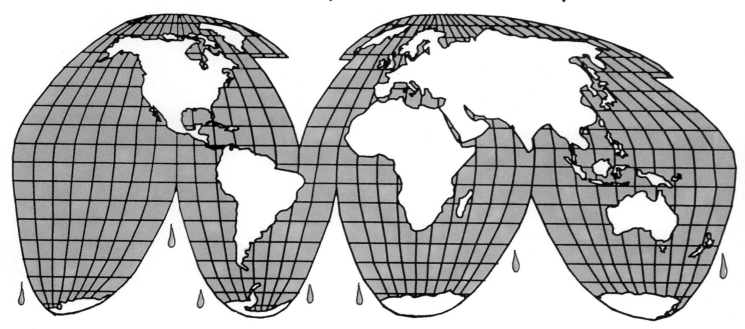

About 70 percent of the surface, or 57,259,000 square miles. Land covers less than one third of the planet's surface. By comparison, the U.S. covers only 2 percent of Earth's surface.

Do hurricanes always spin in the same direction?

That depends on where you are. In the Northern Hemisphere, hurricanes spin in a counterclockwise direction. In the Southern Hemisphere, the same type of storm, called a cyclone, spins clockwise. That is the *Coriolis* force at work. It is caused by the rotation of Earth, which forces things moving freely across Earth's surface to move on a curved path—including wind and ocean currents.

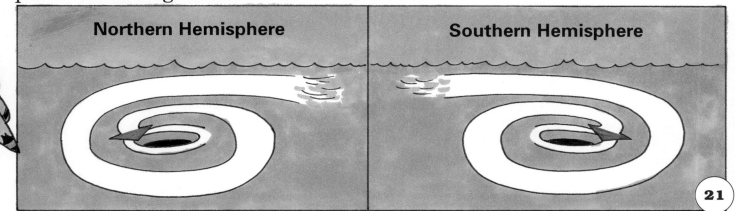

Northern Hemisphere

Southern Hemisphere

Did anybody hear the Big BANG?

No. Most scientists believe that the universe began about 15 to 20 billion years ago, with a huge explosion known as the Big Bang. All the matter in the universe began spreading outward from the point of the explosion, and it is still expanding today.

What is a light-year?

The distance that light travels in a year: 5,880,000,000,000 (or about 6 trillion) miles. Scientists use light-years to describe the huge distances between objects in space.

What is the brightest star that we can see?

Our sun. It seems brightest because it is so close—only 93 million miles away. Sirius, another star, is about 23 times brighter than the sun but much farther away—8.6 light-years. Sirius is also larger and hotter than our sun.

How much would you weigh on the moon?

Someone who weighs 100 pounds on Earth would weigh only 17 pounds on the moon. That is because the moon has a low force of gravity. On Jupiter, which has the strongest gravity of all the planets, that same Earthling would weigh a hefty 260 pounds!

Check Your Weight in Space!

To find out how much you would weigh on another planet, multiply your weight by the planet's force of gravity. For example, a 100-pound weight on Earth would weigh 120 pounds on Saturn: 100 x 1.2 = 120.

Mercury	0.28	Jupiter	2.6
Venus	0.85	Saturn	1.2
Earth	1.0	Uranus	1.1
Mars	0.38	Neptune	1.4
		Pluto	0.03

I FORGOT TO BRING MONEY!

5 ¢

Why do stars twinkle?

Light from stars—other than our own sun—reaches us from so far away that each star looks to us like a tiny point of light. Dust in our atmosphere or even movement of the air makes this little light seem to flicker.

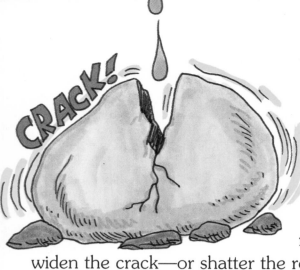

CRACK!

How can water break rocks?

When water freezes, its molecules expand. So if water gets into a crack in a rock, then turns to ice, it can widen the crack—or shatter the rock entirely. Over thousands of years, this process can turn huge mountains into hilly mounds of gravel. The pressure frozen water exerts on a rock is equal to that of an elephant standing on a postage stamp!

I'M A STAMP-STOMPING PACHYDERM!

What is hard water?

Hard water has calcium salts, magnesium salts, iron, and aluminum dissolved in it. The more minerals dissolved in water, the "harder" it is. The harder the water, the more soap you need to work up a lather. Too many minerals dissolved in water can make it taste bad, or unsafe to drink.

PHOOEY!

UGH!

READER, COULD YOU KINDLY FETCH ME 30 GALLONS OF WATER—NOW?

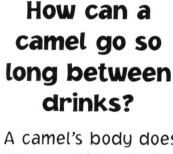

How can a camel go so long between drinks?

A camel's body does a great job storing water. Camels don't sweat much, and their droppings are dry. A thirsty camel can drink 30 gallons of water in 10 minutes! They also get water from desert plants they eat. All liquid is stored in thick body tissues. When water is scarce, camels use the stored water—losing up to 40 percent of their weight.

WHY DOES STILL WATER ACT LIKE A MIRROR?

ACT LIKE A MIRROR?
WHY DOES STILL WATER

All surfaces reflect light. If a surface is smooth and shiny, like still water or a mirror, the light is reflected in an even, orderly way, resulting in a clear image. If the surface is rough, the reflected rays are scattered in different directions, so we don't see a reflected image.

What makes a dry road look wet on a hot day?

Light. What looks like a puddle of water is actually a reflection of the sky. Light rays traveling through cooler air in the sky bend where they meet hot, moist air rising off the road. When light bends, it casts an image of the sky onto the road, just like a mirror.

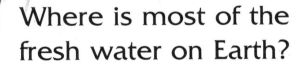

NICE ICE!

Where is most of the fresh water on Earth?

The ice sheet of Antarctica holds 80 to 90 percent of Earth's fresh water—frozen solid. That ice sheet is an average of 7,100 feet thick! (At its thickest point, it is 3 miles deep!) If it ever melted, the sea level around the world would rise by 180 to 200 feet.

Who were the first people to notice the island of Surtsey being born?

Fishermen. One day in 1963, they noticed something that looked like a rock in the ocean near Iceland where rocks had not been before. A volcano was erupting there, under the sea. As the lava spilled and cooled into rock, it piled higher and wider. Only four days after Iceland's brand-new island first poked out of the ocean, it was 200 feet high and 2,000 feet long! Today its diameter is 2,500 feet.

HOW DO VOLCANOES CAUSE COLORFUL SUNSETS?

Volcanoes often pump large amounts of fine ash into the atmosphere. The ash increases the scattering of sunlight, spreading more red and orange light across the sky. This is especially noticeable at sunset and sunrise, when the sky becomes much more red and purple than usual.

What is a tsunami?

A series of giant waves caused by an undersea earthquake or landslide. A tsunami (soo-NAH-mee) may be only three feet high in open sea, but by the time it reaches land it can loom as high as 100 feet. Traveling at speeds up to 450 miles an hour, it can sweep away buildings and cars, even destroy entire towns. The **crest** (top) of a tsunami is known as a tidal wave.

What caused a big boom in 1883?

The volcano of Krakatoa in Indonesia. Eruptions began on August 26, but the biggest explosion came the next day, when nearly the entire island was blown to bits. Steam and ash shot 34 miles into the air, and tsunamis sank ships and killed at least 36,000 people. People could hear the explosion almost 3,000 miles away.

What is a geyser?

A hole in the ground from which steam, gas, and hot water spray into the air. Geysers occur in volcanic areas. **Magma** (melted rock from Earth's core) rises close to the surface, where it heats rocks. Those rocks heat water pooled underground. As that water reaches the boiling point, pressure builds until it shoots from the ground.

WHERE DO YOU FIND STALACTITES AND STALAGMITES?

In limestone caves. They are spikelike rock formations caused by dripping water that deposits minerals. Here's a trick to tell which is which: A stalactite (with a *c*) grows down from the ceiling. A stalagmite (with a *g*) grows up from the ground.

What are atoms?

Tiny building blocks of matter. Every atom is made of some combination of protons, neutrons, and electrons. Atoms of similar structure make up elements such as oxygen, hydrogen, and helium. These are found in nature, and often team up with other elements to form entirely new substances such as water. Two atoms of hydrogen and one atom of oxygen, for instance, make one molecule of water.

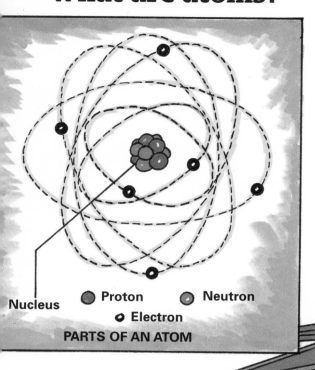

Nucleus

Proton　　**Neutron**

Electron

PARTS OF AN ATOM

HYDROGEN ATOMS

OXYGEN ATOM

What causes radioactivity?

Radioactivity is the energy given off by unstable atoms as they change to a more stable form. This energy can be in the form of heat or light. (The light may not be visible to the human eye.)

What is a nebula?

A gigantic cloud in space, made of gas and dust. A nebula (NEB-yoo-luh) can be dark or bright, depending on whether the particles it contains absorb light or reflect it. Some nebulae are bright because they contain hydrogen and helium gases, which glow. Scientists think that nebulae eventually condense to form stars.

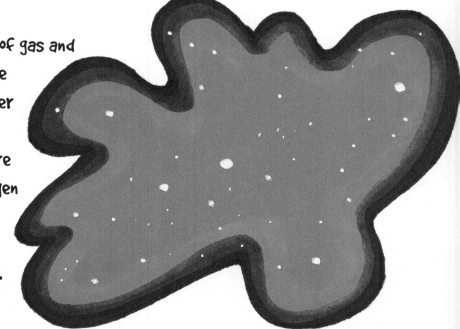

How does the sun make light?

By changing lots of hydrogen to helium. Incredibly high temperatures and pressures at the sun's center set off a fusion reaction: Four hydrogen atoms cram together to make one helium atom. But not all the hydrogen is used. Leftovers are converted to a form of heat and light energy that we call sunshine.

WHAT IS SOLAR WIND?

Bits of atoms—electrons, protons, and some nuclei (NOO-klee-eye)—that the sun's heat speeds up, until they are moving so fast that they escape from the sun's gravity and stream outward. Did you know that a comet's tail always points away from the sun? That is because it is being pushed by solar winds!

STOP PUSHING!

Is Saturn the only planet with rings?

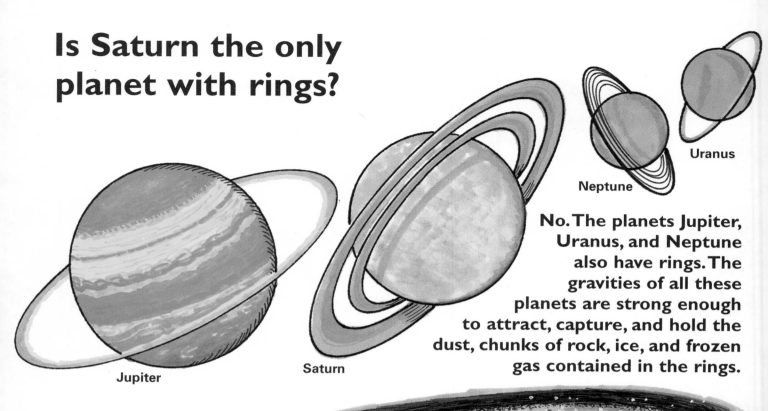

Neptune

Uranus

Jupiter

Saturn

No. The planets Jupiter, Uranus, and Neptune also have rings. The gravities of all these planets are strong enough to attract, capture, and hold the dust, chunks of rock, ice, and frozen gas contained in the rings.

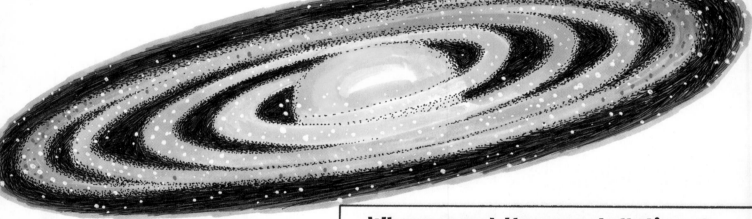

What is the Milky Way?

Our home galaxy. We live in the Milky Way galaxy, a flat, spiral galaxy about 100,000 light-years across. It contains about 200 billion stars—one of which is our sun. Earth is located about 30,000 light-years from the galaxy's center. When we see the hazy band of light called the Milky Way in the night sky, we are seeing the edge of our galaxy.

Who named the constellations?

Ever since people first thought that they could recognize shapes in groups of stars, they have been naming those groups of stars, or constellations. Different cultures use different names for the same constellations. Most of the names that we use, such as Andromeda and Orion, are those of characters in Greek and Roman myths.

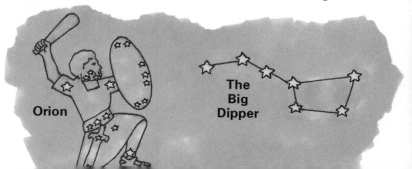

Orion

The Big Dipper

When is Halley's comet coming back?

In the year 2061. The orbit of this famous comet, named after English astronomer Edmond Halley, brings it close to the sun and Earth about every 76 years. Its last appearance was in 1986. American writer Mark Twain was born in 1835 when the comet was in the sky—and died in 1910 on the comet's next visit.

What is an eclipse?

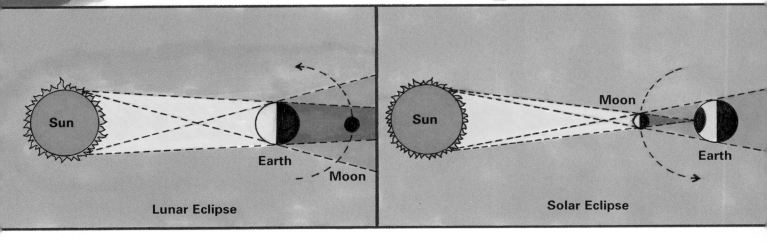

Lunar Eclipse

Solar Eclipse

There are two kinds of eclipses.
*A **lunar eclipse** happens when Earth moves between the moon and the sun, casting Earth's shadow on the moon, which makes it seem to disappear.*
*A **solar eclipse** occurs when the moon passes between Earth and the sun, blocking our view of the sun. The moon's shadow falls on Earth, making the sky dark during the day. For people inside that shadow, the sun seems to disappear.*

Why does the ocean have tides?

As Earth rotates, the moon's gravity tugs on the waters, creating a bulge on each side of Earth. When that bulge occurs near us, we see it as a high tide.
When water has flowed away toward bulges elsewhere, we have a low tide. (There are two high tides and two low tides each day.) The highest tides, called spring tides, happen when the sun and the moon line up, both pulling in the same direction.

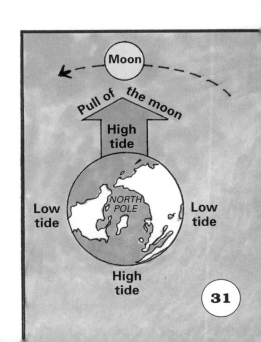

What happens along the U.S. Continental Divide?

Water flows toward either the Atlantic Ocean or the Pacific Ocean. The Continental Divide is an imaginary line in the Rocky Mountains that marks where drainage changes from Pacific-bound rivers on the west side of the line, and Atlantic-bound rivers on the east.

Why does some snow make better snowballs than others?

Snowflakes that form at temperatures close to freezing are bigger and wetter than those that form when temperatures are colder than freezing. Wetter snow is stickier than drier snow, so it makes better snowballs— and snowmen!

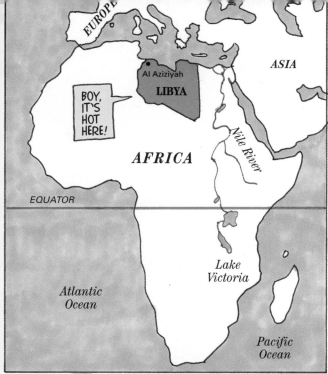

Where is the hottest place on Earth?

On September 13, 1922, the thermometer read 136 degrees Fahrenheit in Al Aziziyah, Libya. (Actually, it read 57.7 degrees Celsius.)

What is the world's longest river?

Either the Amazon of South America or the Nile of Africa, depending on how you measure them. The Nile is generally considered the longest, measuring 4,160 miles from its source to the Mediterranean Sea. The Amazon has many different channels as it nears the Atlantic Ocean, but its length is usually given as 4,000 miles.

WHAT IS THE WORLD'S SUNNIEST PLACE?

The South Pole during summertime in the Antarctic. All that sunshine doesn't melt the snow and ice, because the ice and snow reflect 50 to 90 percent of it right back into space. It doesn't get very warm there, either—it rarely reaches 32 degrees Fahrenheit, even on a "hot" summer day.

Where can you find black smokers and giant tube worms?

Under the sea. Black smokers are big vents on the deep-ocean floor—about 8,000 feet down—that pump out extra-hot water and chemicals. Living near the smokers are some weird animals, including giant tube worms up to 5 feet long.

I'M A GULPER EEL. I LIVE DOWN HERE, TOO!

Can you find a mermaid's purse on the beach?

AH! THERE'S MY PURSE!

Yes. *Mermaid's purse* is the name for leathery rectangular cases that hold the eggs of skates, rays, and dogfish. The cases protect the eggs for six to nine months until they hatch. Purses found on the beach are usually empty.

ASIA

North Pacific Ocean

GUAM

Mariana Trench

EQUATOR

PAPUA NEW GUINEA

Timor Sea

Great Barrier Reef

South Pacific Ocean

AUSTRALIA

How DEEP is the ocean?

The deepest ocean, the Pacific, averages about 13,740 feet in depth. The Mariana Trench, in the Pacific Ocean near Guam, is the deepest spot in that ocean—35,840 feet deep. That's more than 6 miles down!

THANKS, MR. COUSTEAU!

WHO WAS JACQUES-YVES COUSTEAU?

Cousteau (1910-1997) was a French inventor, oceanographer, and filmmaker. In 1943, he and engineer Emile Gagnan invented the aqualung, gear that allows divers to stay underwater for long periods of time. His films about undersea life helped millions of people around the world appreciate the beauty and value of the undersea world—and understand the importance of preserving it.

What deadly hunter lives inside a beautiful seashell?

The cone snail. This soft-bodied animal, which lives inside a shell, shoots a poison-tipped tooth into its prey. Poison from some of the larger cone snails is strong enough to kill humans.

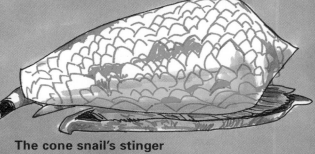

The cone snail's stinger sticks out of its shell.

Why are fish slimy?

For protection. The slippery slime makes it tough for parasites to hook on to a fish's body. Slime also protects fish from harmful bacteria, fungi, and algae. Fish continually make new slime and shed the old, along with any nasty things stuck in it.

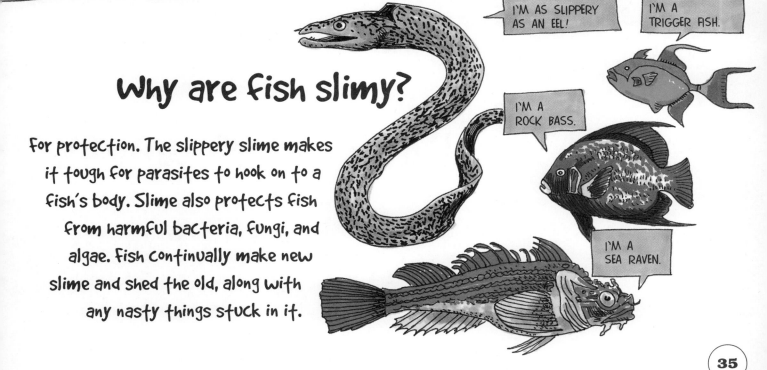

I'M AS SLIPPERY AS AN EEL!

I'M A TRIGGER FISH.

I'M A ROCK BASS.

I'M A SEA RAVEN.

HOW LARGE IS THE BIGGEST FISH?

The biggest fish in the world is the whale shark. It grows up to 40 feet long (or slightly longer)! Don't worry, though—it doesn't eat people. It uses its thousands of tiny teeth to eat small plants, shrimp, and fish.

What do grunion do at night on California beaches?

On certain spring and summer nights, grunion—a kind of small silvery fish—ride the waves onto the beach. Between waves, the females lay eggs in the sand and the males fertilize them. Then the fish ride the next wave out. The eggs hatch 15 days later, when there is another tide high enough to carry the young grunion away.

WHAT CAUSES WAVES?

Usually, wind blowing over the water. The stronger the wind, or the bigger the stretch of water it blows over, the bigger the waves will be. Tides and earthquakes can also stir up water to make waves.

Whose eerie song might you hear in the ocean?

A humpback whale's. A humpback's song sounds like roars, squawks, and sighs to the human ear. A single song can last 30 minutes, and some parts are repeated—just like choruses in our songs. Songs sung by Atlantic humpback whales are different from those of their Pacific relatives.

How much salt is in the ocean?

We don't know, exactly—but scientists estimate that if you took all the salt from the oceans and spread it evenly, it would form a 500-foot-thick layer over the entire Earth.

Is there a fish that uses a fishing rod?

Yes. The anglerfish uses one to do its fishing deep in the ocean. Growing from its forehead is a thin rod that ends in a glowing bump. The anglerfish sits still and jiggles that lure. Any fish that investigates the lure is quickly gulped down. Some anglerfish can even pull their lure close to their mouth for easier chomping!

YOU SHOULD HAVE SEEN THE ONE THAT GOT AWAY!

Why are some clouds light and others dark?

Clouds are made of water vapor—tiny droplets of water. The larger the droplets, the darker the cloud. That's why storm clouds are so dark. They're packed with rain! But even the whitest clouds have gray parts caused by shadows.

IF YOU LIKE THE SOUND OF RAIN, WHERE WOULD BE A GOOD PLACE TO LIVE?

IT'S STILL RAINING.

You might try Mawsynram, India: An average of 467.5 inches of rain falls there every year! Tutunendo, Colombia, would be another choice; it gets 463.4 inches annually. And one year, Cherrapunji, India, was soaked with 1,041.75 inches of rain! (That's higher than an eight-story building!)

Are raindrops really shaped like teardrops?

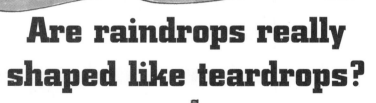

No. No matter how we often see raindrops drawn that way, the real thing looks quite different. A raindrop looks more like a doughnut or bagel in which the hole doesn't go all the way through. The surface tension of water makes it take this shape.

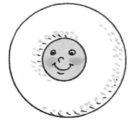

What is hail?

Hail forms when water droplets are repeatedly swept upward into the cold part of storm clouds where they freeze, then drop back down to pick up more moisture. It takes strong winds to keep hailstones circulating in storm clouds.

CAN I BORROW YOUR SCARF?

OUCH!

How BIG can hailstones get?

WOW!

Most are less than half an inch across, but some can be the size of softballs or larger. The largest hailstone on record, which fell in Bangladesh in 1986, weighed 2.25 pounds!

Do any plants eat meat?

Yes, but they gobble bugs, not humans. The Venus's-flytrap and other meat-eaters sprout traps that shut when insects trip them. Some trap prey with glue. Others drown insects in slippery-sloped water traps.

Do whales eat big fish?

Most toothed whales eat fish, but their diets do vary. The sperm whale, for instance, eats mainly giant squid, but also fish, octopus, and skate, a relative of the sting ray. The orca gobbles up seals, penguins, and other whales! And many other whales, in particular the huge blue whale, eat tiny shrimplike animals called krill. They certainly eat their fill of krill—up to four tons a day!

How is a snake able to swallow something larger than its head?

The top and bottom of a snake's jaws are held together with ligaments that stretch like rubber bands. The left and right halves of the lower jaw can spread apart, and the whole jaw can drop downward to open the snake's mouth really wide.

How do hummingbirds eat on the fly?

Hummingbirds survive on a high-sugar substance called nectar. To get it, a hummer sticks its long beak down inside a flower, then rolls its long tongue into a tube to suck up the nectar—all the while batting its wings 50 to 75 times a second.

What do bats eat?

Most bats eat flying insects. Some catch fish, snare spiders and scorpions, or even feast on frogs, lizards, birds, and other bats. Fruit is a favorite with some bats, while others eat flower pollen and nectar. The vampire bat, of course, prefers only the blood of its prey.

When a starfish finds food, what does it do?

The starfish shoves its stomach outside its body and over the food. Then it eats and digests the food before pulling its stomach back inside. A starfish eats animals that move very slowly or tend to lie still, such as snails, clams, and oysters.

CAN PORCUPINES THROW THEIR QUILLS?

No. Porcupines often spin around very fast in order to present their quill-filled backsides to an enemy. The quills are loosely attached to the porcupine's skin and barbed at the tip. Just brushing against these tips is enough to get stuck. The average porcupine has 25,000 to 30,000 quills.

WANT A HUG?

Do hedgehogs have quills when they are born?

Sort of. The quills are buried just beneath the baby hedgehog's skin, which is puffed up with fluid so the quills don't poke through. Not long after birth, the baby's body absorbs the fluid and small white quills poke through its skin.

I'M NO BABY!

How hard can a shark bite?

GULP!

YOU WERE TASTY!

The dusky shark can chomp down with the pressure of 18 tons per square inch—the weight of four adult elephants standing on your thumb! That's about 25,000 times more powerful than an average human's bite!

What surprise is waiting for an animal that grabs a bombardier beetle?

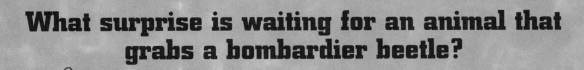

A hot shot. When the bombardier beetle is under attack, chemicals inside its body mix in a special chamber to make a boiling-hot, stinky liquid. The beetle takes aim with its rear end and sprays its attacker.

Why do wasps sting?

BUG OFF!

They are usually saying "leave me alone!" Wasps will sting to defend their nest from predators or anyone else who disturbs it. Some wasps sting caterpillars to paralyze them, then lay their eggs in the caterpillar's flesh. When the tiny wasps hatch, the caterpillar's body provides them with food.

RUN, FEET!

What are the strangler fig's victims?

UGH!

Other plants. Some kinds of fig trees, known as strangler figs, climb up and around other trees, while their roots grow downward. After a while, the fig tree's roots form a thick mat that chokes the life out of the host plant.

WHAT DO SPITTING SPIDERS SPIT?

Something like glue. These spiders spray a sticky, gummy fluid all over their prey, rendering the victim immobile. Splat!

UH-OH!

How does the archerfish get its meals?

UH-OH!

By spitting. This fish lurks underwater, watching for insects on overhanging leaves or grass growing just above the water. When the archerfish spots one, it spits a stream of water droplets, knocking the insect into the water where it can be gobbled up. The fish can shoot a stream five feet high!

PTOOEY!

Which poisonous snake spits?

Africa's spitting cobra. It aims its venom at an enemy's eyes, sometimes shooting while still 10 feet away. The venom either immobilizes the cobra's prey or wards off a potential attacker. If the venom gets in a human's eyes, it causes burning and even temporary blindness.

Do vampire bats really suck blood?

No. Using its razor-sharp teeth, the bat makes a small cut in its prey's skin. The bat licks blood as it oozes from the cut. A chemical in its saliva keeps blood from drying—and numbs skin so victims don't feel a thing. No, vampire bats don't attack humans!

How does a tokay gecko keep its eyes clean?

By licking them. This reptile has no eyelids, so it uses its tongue to moisten and clean its eyes.

Why do snakes stick out their tongues?

A snake's tongue picks up small particles from the air and ground, and carries them to two pits in the roof of the snake's mouth. Nerves in these pits carry smell and taste information about the particles to the snake's brain, helping it identify its surroundings and track prey.

How do diamonds form?

Diamonds are made from carbon, the same element that makes up the graphite in pencil lead. Diamonds form in a kind of rock called kimberlite, about 75 miles below Earth's surface. The tremendous pressure there helps transform it into the crystals known as diamonds. Diamonds are the hardest known natural substance.

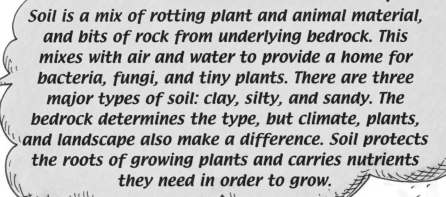

THIS IS NOT WHAT I HAD IN MIND!

Where does soil come from?

Soil is a mix of rotting plant and animal material, and bits of rock from underlying bedrock. This mixes with air and water to provide a home for bacteria, fungi, and tiny plants. There are three major types of soil: clay, silty, and sandy. The bedrock determines the type, but climate, plants, and landscape also make a difference. Soil protects the roots of growing plants and carries nutrients they need in order to grow.

What are the three main kinds of rocks?

Igneous, sedimentary, and metamorphic. Igneous rocks form from **magma** (molten rock). Sedimentary rocks form from layers of sand and mud that settle at the bottom of bodies of water. Metamorphic rocks begin as igneous or sedimentary rocks, but are changed by high temperature and pressure into a new form.

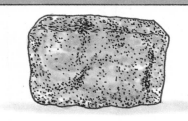

Igneous

Sedimentary

Metamorphic

How **BIG** is the Grand Canyon?

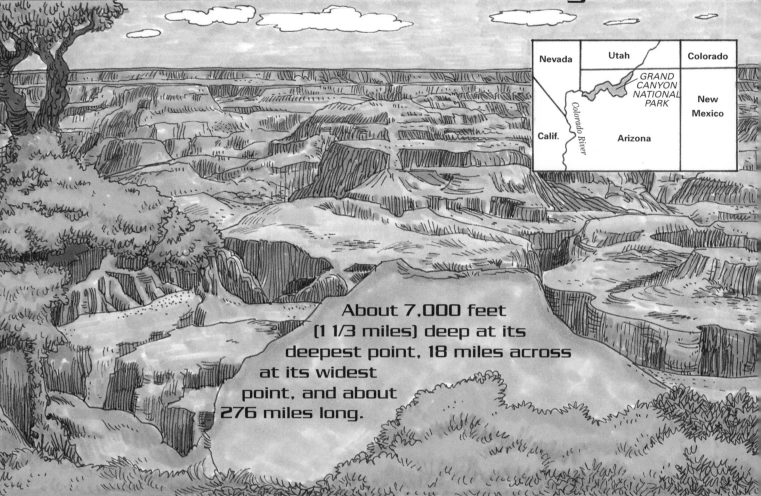

About 7,000 feet (1 1/3 miles) deep at its deepest point, 18 miles across at its widest point, and about 276 miles long.

Will Niagara Falls always exist?

No. The falls exist now because a layer of hard rock called dolomite lies on top of softer rocks, preventing the Niagara River from wearing them away quickly. But as the soft rocks at the base of the falls wear away, the dolomite collapses, causing the falls to move slowly upstream. Eventually, over hundreds of thousands of years—perhaps even millions of years—the falls will disappear into Lake Erie.

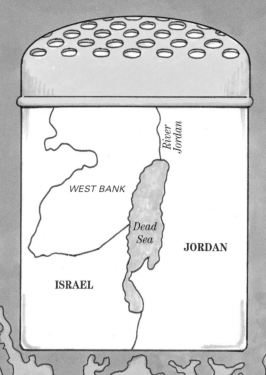

Does anything live in the Dead Sea?

Not much, except for some specialized bacteria and plants. The Dead Sea is really a "terminal" lake—water flows into it, but none flows out. As water evaporates, it leaves behind the salt it contained. The water that is left gets saltier and saltier. The Dead Sea is about eight times as salty as the Atlantic Ocean! By comparison, the Great Salt Lake, in northern Utah, is only three to five times as salty as the ocean.

MMM!

How do coral reefs form?

A coral polyp is a tiny animal that builds a hard outer skeleton. When a polyp dies, it leaves behind its skeleton. Other polyps build on top of it; and still others grow on top of them. In warm, shallow seas over thousands of years, billions of these tiny skeletons form a coral reef.

Where do pearls come from?

Pearls form when foreign matter, such as a piece of sand, gets inside the shell of an oyster or mussel, irritating the animal's soft body. To protect itself, the shellfish coats the object with layers of a smooth, hard substance called nacre (NAY-ker). In time, as layers build up, the coated object becomes a pearl.

OUCH! SAND JUST GOT INSIDE MY SHELL!

Can fish breathe underwater?

Yes. Water passes into a fish's mouth and over its gills. Blood flowing through the gills absorbs oxygen in the water. At the same time, the blood releases carbon dioxide, which is waste, into the water.

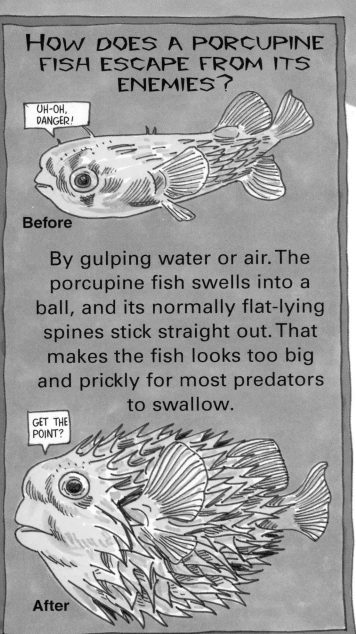

HOW DOES A PORCUPINE FISH ESCAPE FROM ITS ENEMIES?

UH-OH, DANGER!

Before

By gulping water or air. The porcupine fish swells into a ball, and its normally flat-lying spines stick straight out. That makes the fish looks too big and prickly for most predators to swallow.

GET THE POINT?

After

What do dolphins and some bats have in common?

I CAN'T FLY!

I CAN'T SWIM!

Both use echolocation to find their prey. They send out sound waves in the form of high-pitched shrieks, which bounce off objects. Returning echoes tell them the direction and distance of things they can't see. With echolocation, the greater horseshoe bat can catch moths in flight and a dolphin can single out a fish from a whole school of them. Dolphins and some bats also use echolocation to help find their way around.

Are all deserts hot and sandy?

No. A desert is a place that gets less than 10 inches of rain a year, often much less. So a desert may be hot and sandy, but it may also be rocky, dusty, or even very cold—Antarctica, for instance.

Why is xeriscaping a good idea in dry climates?

Xeriscaping (ZEER-uh-SKAPE-ing) is landscaping that doesn't need much water. Xeriscapers use plants that are suited for dry areas, and water them with drip-irrigation systems that lose much less water to evaporation than regular sprinklers do.

Which insects build air-conditioned homes?

Termites. Inside a termite mound, hot air rises into porous-walled chimneys at the top. There, carbon-dioxide waste and heat escape to the outside, while oxygen comes in from the outside. The cooler, oxygenated air sinks into the mound, where the colony lives.

THIS IS GOING TO BE COOL!

WHY DON'T CACTI HAVE LEAVES?

Most plants rely on their leaves to make food, but a plant's water supply can evaporate quickly from a leaf's broad surface. Cacti, which live mainly in areas where water is scarce, have no leaves, but make food in their stems instead. A cactus stem also acts as a water barrel, allowing some large cacti to store tons of water.

Where would you look for living stones?

In the South African desert. A living stone is a type of plant similar to cacti. Each plant has two big, round, swollen, waxy leaves stuck together. The leaves, which are colored like pebbles, blend in with the plant's surroundings.

51

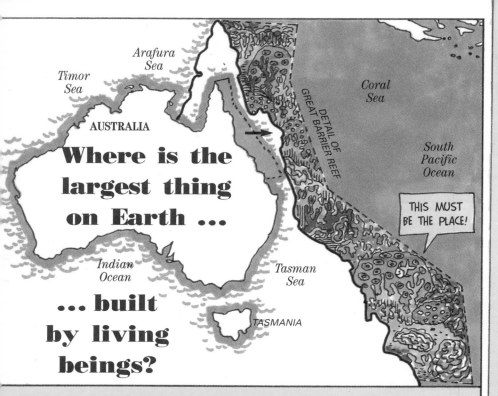

Where is the largest thing on Earth ...

... built by living beings?

THIS MUST BE THE PLACE!

In the sea off the coast of Australia. The Great Barrier Reef, which is made of coral, is **1,250** miles long and occupies about **80,000** square miles.

How do crickets sing?

By rubbing their wings together. One wing has a row of bumps that look like the teeth on a comb; the other wing is edged with tough tissue. When the toughened edge hits a bump, it makes a click that is **amplified** *(made louder) by another part of the wing. Only male crickets sing.*

Are humans the only animals that use tools?

No. Chimpanzees poke twigs into termite nests, then eat the insects that cling to the twig when it is pulled out. Egyptian vultures drop stones on ostrich eggs to break them open. Otters balance stones on their bellies, using them to crack open clams and other shellfish. Other animals use tools, too.

THE SKY IS FALLING?

What does the trap-door spider do with its trapdoor?

When it is hungry, the spider lurks just under the hinged lid to its burrow, out of sight, waiting to grab prey that wander too close. The same trapdoor also protects the spider from becoming another animal's prey.

How do male bowerbirds advertise for mates?

With decorated display sites called bowers. The male builds two parallel walls of sticks, which he may steal from another bird. Then he adds shells, pebbles, bits of glass, even buttons and coins. Blue feathers are the most popular items.

Why do some orchids look like bees?

To fool bees into spreading their pollen. When the bee tries to mate with what it thinks is another bee, some of the orchid's pollen sticks to it. The bee then carries that pollen to other orchids, fertilizing them.

How do PALEOCLIMATOLOGISTS figure out Earth's past climates?

I CAN'T EVEN FIGURE OUT HOW TO PRONOUNCE IT!*

They use many kinds of clues. Ancient air trapped in Antarctica's ice gives information about the atmosphere long ago. Plant and animal fossils can reveal how warm, cold, wet, or dry it was. Experts called palynologists (pal-ih-NOLL-uh-jists) even study pollen, ancient and modern. By figuring out what plant the tiny fossilized grains came from, palynologists can reconstruct ancient landscapes.

*Simple! Just say, "PAY-lee-oh-KLY-muh-TAHL-uh-jists."

What is the greenhouse effect?

The glass of a greenhouse traps the sun's heat inside. Earth's atmosphere acts like that glass, keeping the planet's surface warmer than it would be otherwise. If it didn't, Earth would be covered with ice. But now scientists worry that we are making it *too* warm. Adding carbon dioxide to the atmosphere, which traps the sun's heat, increases this warming effect. Carbon dioxide gas is a normal part of the atmosphere, but cars, power plants, and other human-made devices give off much more than would occur naturally.

What are glaciers?

I LOVE THIS KIND OF WEATHER!

Glaciers are big, slowly moving masses of ice, often found in mountain valleys. They move from higher to lower elevations until finally the amount of ice melting at their lower end equals the amount of new snow being added on top. As they move, glaciers can carve out valleys, cut off hills, and reshape landscapes.

WHAT WERE THE ICE AGES?

The Ice Ages were periods in prehistoric times when vast sheets of ice covered many parts of Earth. Glaciers and ice sheets up to 10,000 feet thick covered much of Europe, North America, Asia, and southern Africa. The last Ice Age ended about 10,000 to 14,000 years ago.

Where was the first real weather-recording station?

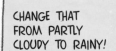

CHANGE THAT FROM PARTLY CLOUDY TO RAINY!

Oxford, England. The Radcliffe Observatory there began keeping regular, daily weather records in January 1815, tracking the area's temperature and rainfall. The Radcliffe's archives include older weather records; irregular readings were taken there as far back as 1767.

What happens to a mercury thermometer at -40°F and below?

It becomes useless, because the mercury freezes. To measure temperatures colder than -40°F, scientists use thermometers filled with alcohol, or ones that measure the movement of electrons.

Why does it take longer to hard-boil an egg in Denver than in New Orleans?

Water's boiling point is strongly affected by air pressure, which is lower at high altitudes. The lower the pressure, the more molecules can expand and spread out. As a result, at these high altitudes, there is less oxygen in the air and water takes longer to boil. That's why you need more time to boil an egg in Denver, Colorado—nicknamed "the Mile-High City" for its high altitude—than in New Orleans, Louisiana, which is at sea level.

What is the difference between Fahrenheit and Celsius temperatures?

Fahrenheit (F) and Celsius (C) are two different scales that give the same information: the temperature in degrees (°). Water freezes at a certain temperature: 32°F or 0°C. Its boiling point is 212°F or 100°C.

To convert from Fahrenheit to Celsius, take the temperature, subtract 32, multiply by 5, then divide by 9. To convert Celsius to Fahrenheit, multiply the Celsius temperature by 1.8, then add 32.

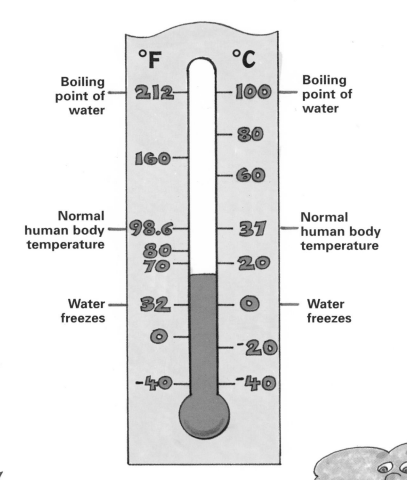

°F	°C	
Boiling point of water — 212	100 — Boiling point of water	
160	80	
	60	
Normal human body temperature — 98.6	37 — Normal human body temperature	
80		
70	20	
Water freezes — 32	0 — Water freezes	
0	-20	
-40	-40	

Can counting cricket chirps really help you find out the temperature?

Folklore says yes, but there is no scientific basis for this method. Sometimes it works, sometimes it doesn't! If you want to try it, do this: Count how many times a cricket chirps in 14 seconds, then add 40. That is supposed to give you the temperature in degrees Fahrenheit.

READY, SET, COUNT!

How quickly can the temperature change?

Ask anyone who was in Spearfish, South Dakota, on January 22, 1943. That day, the temperature in Spearfish shot up 49° in just 2 minutes (from -4°F to 45°F). Later that same morning, it fell 58°F (from 54°F to -4°F) in 27 minutes! That weather roller coaster was probably caused by cold and warm fronts bouncing off the Black Hills and across the Great Plains.

I'M WARM!

I'M COLD!

57

What happened to passenger pigeons?

About 200 years ago, some three to five billion passenger pigeons lived in North America. They were overhunted by humans, however, and became extinct. The last passenger pigeon, named Martha, died in 1914. This may have been the only time in history when humans witnessed the precise moment of a species' extinction.

Why did Congress pass the Endangered Species Act?

To protect plants and animals threatened by human activities. This law, passed in 1973, makes any activity that threatens the survival of an endangered species illegal. In North America alone, more than 900 plants and animals are considered endangered.

THANKS FOR PUTTING THE ROCKY MOUNTAIN GOAT ON THE LIST!

Who was John Muir?

Scottish-born John Muir (1838-1914) was one of America's earliest conservationists. He explored California's Sierra Nevada Mountains and Alaska's glaciers, and used his writings to teach people about nature's beauty. At his urging, the U.S. government established Yosemite and Sequoia national parks. Muir also founded the Sierra Club, an organization that continues to support conservation today.

WHAT IS A FOOD CHAIN?

Eaters being eaten by other eaters. Food chains usually begin with plants, which make their own food. Animals eat the plants, then are eaten by other animals, which are eaten by other animals, and so on. Any break in a food chain can be disastrous to many types of life. For instance, if prairie dogs are killed off by habitat destruction, ferrets that eat prairie dogs will dwindle in number, too. Many different food chains are part of larger food webs—several food chains linked together—because most animals eat more than one kind of food.

YUM YUM YUM YUM YUM YUM

Where was the first national park?

In an area that spreads across parts of Idaho, Montana, and Wyoming. In 1872, U.S. President Theodore Roosevelt and the U.S. Congress made this area, named Yellowstone National Park, the first national park in the U.S.—and the world. Today, the U.S. National Park Service oversees 54 national parks, as well as a number of historic sites, seashores, memorials, and other protected sites.

Why are so many animals in danger of becoming extinct?

I'M A TUATARA!

I'M AN ARCTIC FOX.

Many of the things that humans have built—cities, roads, automobiles, and power plants, for instance—pollute or limit the habitats of animals. The numbers of some wild species are also reduced by hunting. Threatened species have been saved when people have made an effort to change destructive habits.

I'M A JAGUAR.

What are fossil fuels?

Fuels made from the remains of plants that lived millions of years ago. Natural gas, coal, and oil are all fossil fuels.

What is acid rain?

Rain tainted by **toxic** (poisonous) chemicals. Acid rain is formed when gases given off by the burning of coal, gasoline, or oil rise into the air and mix with water vapor in the clouds, making it acidic. When this falls as rain, it pollutes lakes and rivers. If the acidity gets too high, it kills fish and plants. It also can damage building materials, such as limestone, marble, and bronze.

What is the ozone layer?

A section of Earth's atmosphere, between 9 and 25 miles above Earth's surface. Ozone, a gas made of molecules containing three oxygen atoms, is a natural part of Earth's atmosphere. The ozone layer is important to life on Earth because it absorbs harmful ultraviolet rays coming from the sun. Scientists fear human activity has damaged this layer, allowing more damaging sunlight to penetrate our atmosphere.

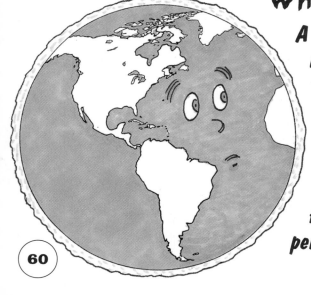

Who was Rachel Carson?

Rachel Carson (1907-1964) was a marine biologist and environmentalist. In 1962, her book *Silent Spring* was published and gained widespread attention. It made many people aware, for the first time, of how humans were polluting the environment with insecticides. Carson wrote other nature books, but *Silent Spring* is regarded as her masterpiece—the book that launched the modern environmental movement throughout the world.

How can pesticides harm birds?

If a bird eats animals that have been exposed to pesticides, the chemicals stay in the bird's body and become concentrated there. Sometimes these chemicals cause a bird to lay eggs with shells that break easily, preventing the eggs from hatching. If the bird absorbs too high a level of the chemicals, it may be poisoned and die. Pesticides almost wiped out peregrine falcons and bald eagles in the eastern U.S.

PESTICIDES RUINED MY EGGS!

What is organic gardening?

A way of growing plants without using chemical pesticides and fertilizers. *Organic* means using natural food or fertilizers rather than chemical ones. Organic fertilizers, such as **compost** (rotted plant material) or fishmeal, are used to enrich the soil. Instead of an insecticide, an organic farmer may use ladybugs to get rid of problem insects. Organic gardening grows crops without hurting the environment.

What is dew?

On cool, cloud-free nights, if the temperature of the ground and other surfaces drops low enough, warm air cools down, condensing moisture contained in it. That moisture collects on cool surfaces in droplets of water called dew.

Why does the Namibian darkling beetle stand on its head?

I'M THIRSTY!

The Namibian darkling beetle lives in the desert, where water is scarce. As it stands on its head, moisture from damp breezes condenses on its shell, forming dewdrops. The drops trickle down to the beetle's mouth, and it drinks them.

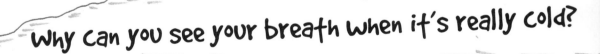

Why can you see your breath when it's really cold?

When you exhale in cold weather, the water vapor in your warm breath hits the cold air and condenses into tiny water droplets. Presto: an instant mini-cloud!

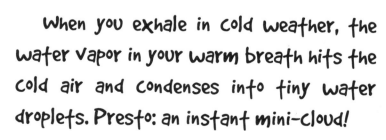

HOW DID YOU DO THAT?

What is the driest place on Earth?

The Atacama Desert in northern Chile. It gets almost no rainfall, except for an occasional shower only several times each century. Rain falls so seldom there that the showers average out to a mere 0.003 inches of rain a year. Now *that* is dry! Another very dry place is the area around the South Pole, in Antarctica. What little moisture there is is locked up solid—frozen into ice.

WE NEVER GO THERE!

South Atlantic Ocean

IF YOU'RE GOING TO VISIT HERE, BRING YOUR OWN WATER!

ATACAMA DESERT

C H I L E

South Pacific Ocean

How can a sponge hold water if it's got holes?

The holes in a sponge expose more of the sea creature's absorbent surface, letting it soak up far more water than a sponge with no holes ever could. The first sponges people used were the porous bodies of certain sea animals, but humans later learned how to make artificial sponges.

A   B   C

Three Types of Natural Sponge
A. Purple tube
B. Sulphur
C. Sheepswool

Will fool's gold make you rich?

No way. Fool's gold is pyrite, a mineral that contains iron and sulfur. Prospectors were often fooled into thinking that pyrite was gold because it looks metallic and has a golden color. That is how it got its nickname. Geologists never mistake the two. Gold, one of the heaviest metals, can be pounded into other shapes, stretched into wire, and cut into slices. Pyrite has none of these properties.

Where does amber come from?

Amber is fossilized sap, or resin, from trees that lived about 40 to 60 million years ago. Sometimes the transparent yellow pieces of amber contain insects, leaves, or parts of other living things that were trapped in the sticky sap before it hardened.

What is petrified wood?

Over thousands of years, water seeping through buried wood slowly replaces parts of the plant with minerals, such as silica and calcium carbonate. This makes the wood look as if it has petrified, or turned to stone. Sometimes this mineralization is so thorough that the ancient wood is preserved with all of its original details intact. The famous Petrified Forest, located in northeastern Arizona, contains fossilized trees 225 million years old.

ATTENTION, FELLOW WOOD-PECKERS ... DO NOT VISIT THE PETRIFIED FOREST!

What is so interesting about the La Brea Tar Pits?

Their record of prehistoric life. Between 10,000 and 40,000 years ago, many animals became trapped in the pools of sticky tar that oozed from below Earth's surface. Bones of saber-toothed tigers, mammoths, horses, and camels have all been found here, along with plant fossils. This ancient site is in the midst of a modern city—Los Angeles, California.

How was coal formed?

Hundreds of millions of years ago, trees and other plants died in ancient swamps and sank into the water, layer upon layer. As the swamplands sank, seas covered them, laying silt and sand, called sediment, over the decaying plants. As layers of sediment built up, pressure on the plant material increased, forcing out the water and pressing together what was left. Over time, this changed the plant matter into coal.

Peat-forming swamp

Compacted sediments and sedimentary rocks

Compressed peat

COAL

Underclay

How do forest fires start?

Often with a lightning strike. The air at a lightning bolt's center is very hot—as much as five times as hot as the surface of the sun. When that heat meets the wood of a dry tree, it sparks a fire that spreads to other trees. Forest fires are also started by careless campers who fail to put out their fires properly.

Was there really a man called Johnny Appleseed?

Yes. His real name was John Chapman (1774-1845). He traveled throughout the U.S. Midwest, planting apple orchards. He also gave seeds and young trees to pioneers who were headed west, encouraging them to plant their own orchards. By the time he died, he owned many plant nurseries and orchards, and had won fame for starting many others.

Why are *RAIN FORESTS* so important?

ANOTHER RAINY DAY!

YES!

They provide homes for more than half the known (and unknown) plant and animal species on Earth—more than any other habitat. Rain forests grow medicinal plants and rid the air of pollutants. But sadly, humans have cut down much of them. Today the forests cover only two percent of Earth's surface; once, they covered twice that area. The forests are in Central and South America, West and Central Africa, and Southeast Asia.

Who was Smokey the Bear?

ONLY **YOU** CAN PREVENT FOREST FIRES.

At first, he was just a cartoon character that told people, "Only *you* can prevent forest fires." Then, in 1950, a fire-fighting crew in New Mexico rescued a bear cub from a forest fire. Named Smokey after the cartoon, he lived at the National Zoo in Washington, D.C., serving as a symbol for fire prevention. Smokey died in 1976.

How are fish scales like tree trunks?

I'M BIG!

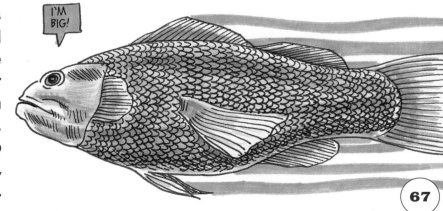

Both grow more in spring and summer than in winter. This seasonal growth can be used to calculate fish ages. Fine ridges on the scales are closer in lean years, farther apart in years of abundant food. Scientists can use them to track Earth's cycle of floods, droughts, and diseases.

67

HOW MANY KINDS OF INSECTS ARE THERE?

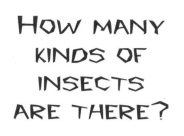

We know of about 750,000 to 1,000,000 species, but there are probably at least that many species that haven't been discovered yet. However, habitat destruction, especially of the rain forests, is wiping out many species before we have a chance to learn about them or even know that they exist.

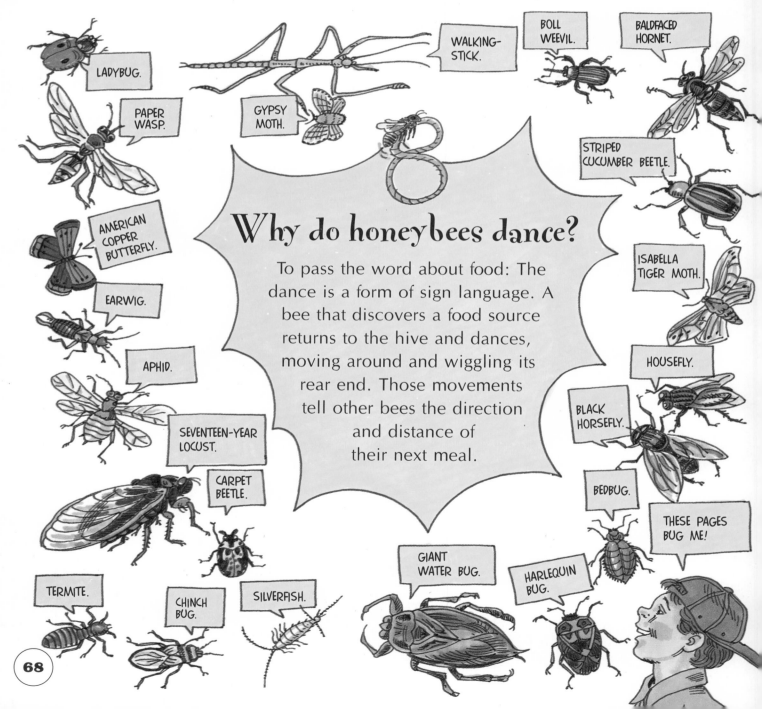

Why do honeybees dance?

To pass the word about food: The dance is a form of sign language. A bee that discovers a food source returns to the hive and dances, moving around and wiggling its rear end. Those movements tell other bees the direction and distance of their next meal.

Is there an insect that eats animal dung?

Yes, the aptly named dung beetle. Dung beetles live all over the world—just about anywhere animal dung is found. There are thousands of different species; most eat the dung. Some species roll it into a big ball and lay their eggs in it. It sounds yucky, but dung beetles are vitally important. They help keep planet Earth clean!

Where do dragonflies live until they get their wings?

BEATS ME!

Under water. Young dragonflies, called nymphs (NIMFS), have gills and can breathe underwater. Nymphs are great hunters; they will even capture small frogs or fish. After **molting** (shedding its skin) several times under the water, the nymph climbs out of the water, sheds its skin one last time, and emerges as an adult dragonfly.

Why are some insects born without a mouth?

Because they don't need one! Some male moths live only long enough to mate before dying. They don't have a mouth because eating would waste the precious time they have to further their species.

Which is stronger, spiderweb silk or steel?

Spiderweb silk! You have to pull harder to break a strand of silk than you do to break a steel wire of the same thickness.

What happened at Silver Lake, Colorado, in 1921?

It snowed 76 inches in a single, 24-hour-period! It was not even winter then—that incredible snowfall occurred in the middle of April!

Almost as bad was the 24-hour snowfall that hit Thompson Pass, Alaska, on December 29, 1955: 62 inches.

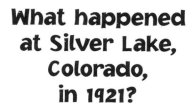

I DID NOT KNOW THAT!

What helps the little Arctic fox keep warm?

Its fur, for starters. Arctic fox fur insulates better than that of any other mammal. This fox's short legs, furry feet, and small, round ears help reduce the loss of heat from its body. The Arctic fox's body doesn't have to start working harder to keep it warm until the temperature drops below -40°F.

LISTEN TO THIS!

WHY DOES SNOW SOMETIMES SQUEAK?

When the temperature is 20°F or colder, soft, wet snowflakes turn into hard, rough ice crystals. The squeaking that you hear when you step on the snow is the sound of thousands of those crystals bumping into and sliding past each other.

What happens during an AVALANCHE?

Tons of snow slide down a steep slope. It takes very little to trigger an avalanche: A change of temperature, the weight of new snow, even the weight of a single skier or the slam of a car door can set one off. An avalanche can move faster than 200 miles an hour, burying everything in its path.

Where is it colder, at the North Pole or the South Pole?

North Pole

BRRRR!

South Pole

The South Pole. It sits on a mountain, where it is colder than at sea level. The North Pole is located on an ice cap floating on the Arctic Ocean. Warmth from the ocean keeps the North Pole's temperature higher than it would be otherwise.

What are pingos?

Soil-covered mounds of ice found in permafrost areas in the Arctic and the interior of Alaska. A pingo is usually circular and may be up to 230 feet tall. At its center is a core of almost pure ice. In Eskimo, pingo means "small hill."

How hard can the wind blow?

We don't know the absolute limit, but a world-record gust of 231 miles per hour was once recorded at the observatory on Mount Washington, New Hampshire. People there are used to breezy days—they regularly get 100 mile-an-hour winds.

What is a CYCLONE?

A tropical storm spiraling around a clear, central area called the eye. Only storms with winds higher than 74 miles per hour are called tropical cyclones. This type of storm, found in warm areas, is called a hurricane when it occurs in the Atlantic Ocean or Caribbean Sea; a typhoon when it occurs in the western Pacific. A tropical cyclone may be 600 miles across and carry hundreds of thunderstorms.

Who started naming hurricanes?

I'LL NAME THIS ONE AFTER ME!

For centuries, hurricanes in the Caribbean area were named for the saint's day when they struck. In the late 19th century, Clement Wragge, an Australian meteorologist, started giving hurricanes women's names. Since 1979, the names have been taken from an alphabetical list of both male and female names chosen each year by an international meteorological committee.

WHY DOES THE WIND BLOW?

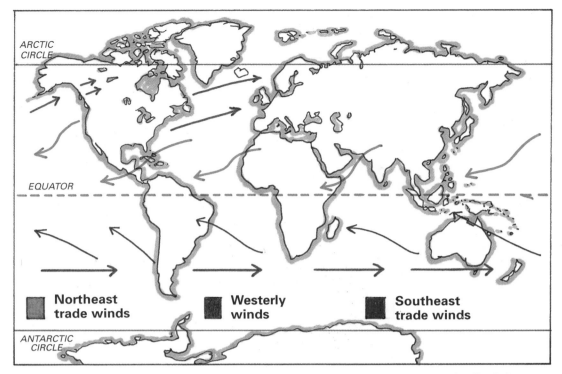

Northeast trade winds

Westerly winds

Southeast trade winds

Because not all the air on Earth is the same temperature. Warm air is lighter than cold air. As warm air rises, cool air flows in to take its place. This movement is what we call wind—nature's way of evenly mixing hot and cold air.

What is a tornado?

A violently spinning column of air, which touches the ground while hanging from a parent storm cloud. A tornado usually lasts only minutes, causing damage in a small area. Some, however, keep going for hours, traveling and wreaking havoc for hundreds of miles. Wind speed in the most violent tornadoes can reach as high as 300 miles per hour!

What makes flamingoes pink?

Flamingoes get their color from pigments in the food they eat, which includes small fish, insects, and algae. These are similar to the pigments that tint carrots and tomatoes. Flamingoes in zoos may turn white if they are not given the right kind of food.

> WHAT DO FLAMINGO LAWN ORNAMENTS EAT?

What makes grass green?

> IT SURE IS GREEN!

Chlorophyll (KLOR-uh-fill), a bright-green substance found in leaves. Grass, trees, and other leaf-bearing plants use chlorophyll to turn sunlight into energy, in a process called photosynthesis (FOH-toh-SIN-thuh-sis). This is what provides plants with the food they need to grow.

What makes some animals' eyes shine at night?

Animals that are active at night, such as cats, wolves, and owls, have a shiny layer at the back of their eyes that reflects light upon the part of the eye where images are formed. This lets animals see in very low light. The shine that we see is light reflecting off that layer.

How do chameleons change color?

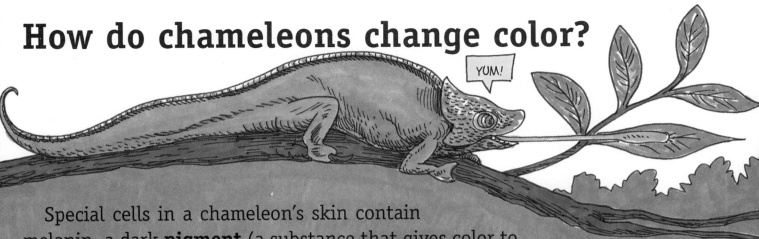

Special cells in a chameleon's skin contain melanin, a dark **pigment** (a substance that gives color to plant and animal cells). When the melanin is confined tightly in the cell, the lizard is light-colored. When the melanin expands, the chameleon darkens. A chameleon's color can change according to its body temperature and mood.

Are all white animals albinos?

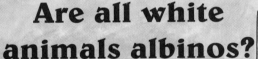

No. True albino animals are white because they lack melanin. Their eyes are pink due to the blood coursing through them. Other animals may be almost entirely white but still have melanin in some areas, such as their noses or eyes.

Why are poisonous animals often brightly colored?

Bright colors work like warning signs that say, "Keep off! I'm dangerous!" to potential predators. If an animal *is* lucky enough to survive eating or attacking one of these creatures, it will always remember that bright colors make for an unpleasant experience.

What makes seasons change?

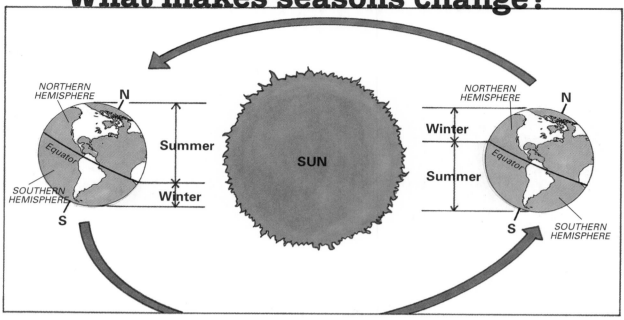

Earth is tilted on its axis, and keeps that tilt as it moves around the sun. When the northern half is tilted toward the sun, it has long, warm summer days, while the south has the short, cool days of winter. On the other side of the sun, the positions are reversed, giving the north winter and the south summer.

Why do leaves change color, then fall from trees in autumn?

Triggered by shorter days and lower temperatures, trees stop making chlorophyll. Chlorophyll's green color normally covers up red and yellow pigments in the leaves. With chlorophyll gone, those colors become visible. In autumn, leaves add cells at their bases that cut them off from the tree's food and water supply. Eventually, the leaves fall off. This seems sad, but it's smart: Winter's reduced sunlight means trees wouldn't be able to grow, feed, and support all those leaves anyway.

What is hibernation?

ZZZZ...

PLEASE DO NOT DISTURB

A strategy to conserve energy when the weather is cold and food is scarce. Some animals, such as black bears, pass each winter curled up asleep in a warm place. Their body temperatures drop and their body processes slow down.

What do snowshoe rabbits and ptarmigan (TAR-mih-gun) do in spring and fall?

Change colors. These animals live in the far north, where winters are long and snowy. As winter approaches, the animals' coloring gradually changes from a mottled brown to a snowy white that blends better with snow. In the spring, it changes back to brown.

Where do butterflies go in winter?

When the weather starts to get chilly, some butterflies, such as the monarch, migrate to warmer places. Butterflies that stay in cold areas hibernate through the winter, after laying eggs. The eggs hatch, and the offspring spend the winter as caterpillars or in cocoons, where the transformation from caterpillar to butterfly occurs.

Does hay cause hay fever?

A·A·A·A·CHOoo!

Not really. The sneezes and sniffles of hay fever are an allergic reaction to pollen and mold in the air. (Allergies make the body's defensive systems react to harmless substances as if they were dangerous.) Hay fever is worst in spring, when flowers bloom, and in autumn, when mold grows on fallen leaves.

Where is the world's tallest waterfall?

On the Churún River, in a rain-forest area of Venezuela, in South America. Angel Falls drops 3,212 feet from the rim of a mesa to the river valley below. Its longest unbroken drop is a 2,648-foot plunge down a sheer cliff.

HOW HIGH IS THE SKY?

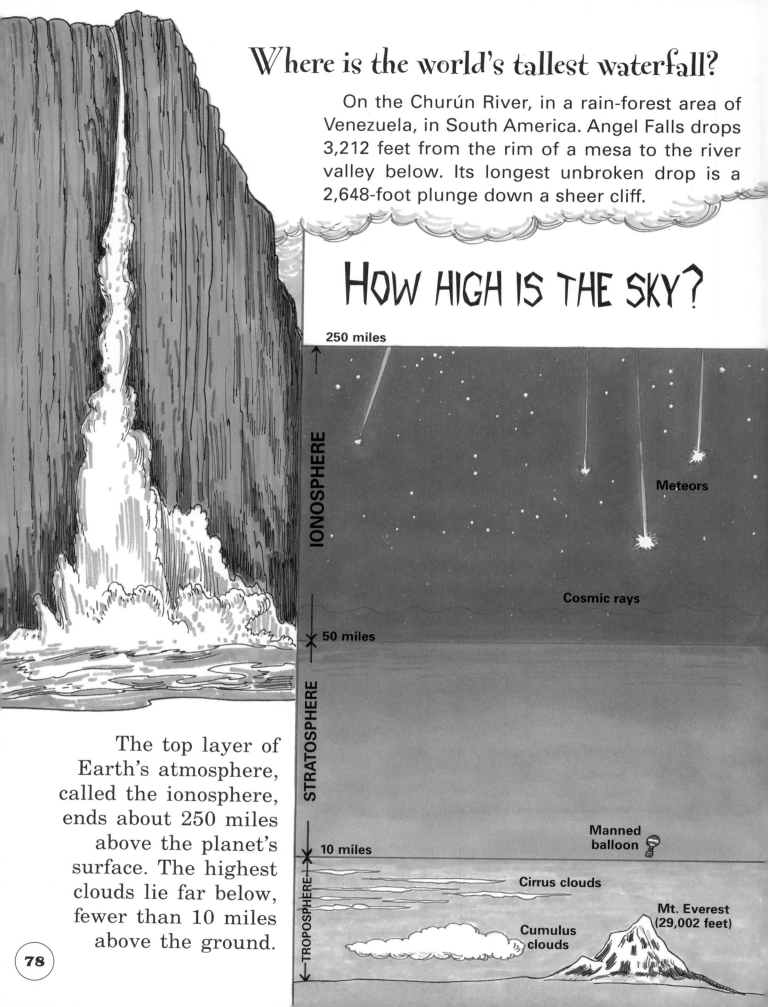

250 miles

IONOSPHERE

Meteors

Cosmic rays

50 miles

STRATOSPHERE

Manned balloon

10 miles

TROPOSPHERE

Cirrus clouds

Mt. Everest (29,002 feet)

Cumulus clouds

The top layer of Earth's atmosphere, called the ionosphere, ends about 250 miles above the planet's surface. The highest clouds lie far below, fewer than 10 miles above the ground.

How fast does a snail move?

When a garden snail is really zipping along, it can manage 0.005 miles (26.4 feet) per hour. Snails crawl on their single foot. A special gland in the foot secretes mucus that lubricates their path.

WHAT'S THE RUSH?

How many ants are there on Earth?

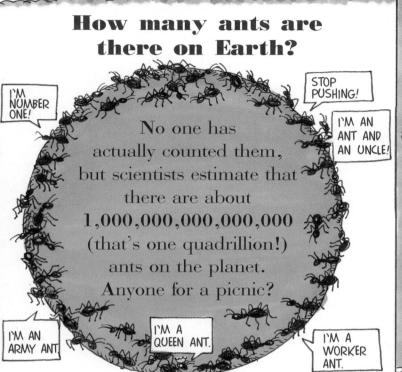

No one has actually counted them, but scientists estimate that there are about 1,000,000,000,000,000 (that's one quadrillion!) ants on the planet. Anyone for a picnic?

I'M NUMBER ONE!

STOP PUSHING!

I'M AN ANT AND AN UNCLE!

I'M AN ARMY ANT

I'M A QUEEN ANT.

I'M A WORKER ANT.

I'M A REAL SENIOR CITIZEN.

What fills the skies over Veracruz, Mexico, each autumn?

Birds. Millions of raptors (birds of prey) pass over Veracruz as they migrate from their northern summer homes to wintering quarters in South America. Almost a million hawks could fly by in a single day.

HERE THEY COME!

Do trees live a very long time?

Some species do. Bristlecone pines found in California may be the oldest trees on Earth. One of them is nearly 5,000 years old—more than 1,000 years older than any other type of tree! Scientists think that it could live for another 1,000! Bristlecones may live a long time, but they don't grow to be very tall—60 feet, at most.

Bilby

Bulbul

What is the difference between a bilby and a bulbul?

A bilby, also known as a rabbit-eared bandicoot, is an Australian marsupial with long, skinny ears, large hind legs, and a bushy tail. A bulbul is one of a family of rather plain-looking Asian and African birds. Bulbuls are busy, noisy birds that grow up to 11 inches long.

What is quicksand?

A very thick liquid formed when water flows through and mixes with sand. Quicksand appears to be firm enough to walk on, but will not support a person's weight. By moving slowly and carefully, a person who has sunk in quicksand can work his or her way to safe ground.

Do woodpeckers get headaches?

TA-TA-TA-TA-TA-TA-TA!!

NOPE, I JUST GIVE THEM!

You might think so, but the answer is no. Big neck muscles support the woodpecker's extra-thick skull, which acts like a built-in crash helmet to absorb the force of its hammering blows. The woodpecker also has stiff tail feathers, which it presses against the tree for support, lessening the impact.

Why do some species of flower smell like rotting flesh?

SOMETHING SMELLS GOOD TO ME!

To attract flies. Plants like the giant rafflesia, or "stinking corpse lily," rely on flies for pollination. The flowers' stinky smell ensures that plenty of flies show up to do the job.

P.U.!

How do pythons, boas, and other constrictor snakes kill their prey?

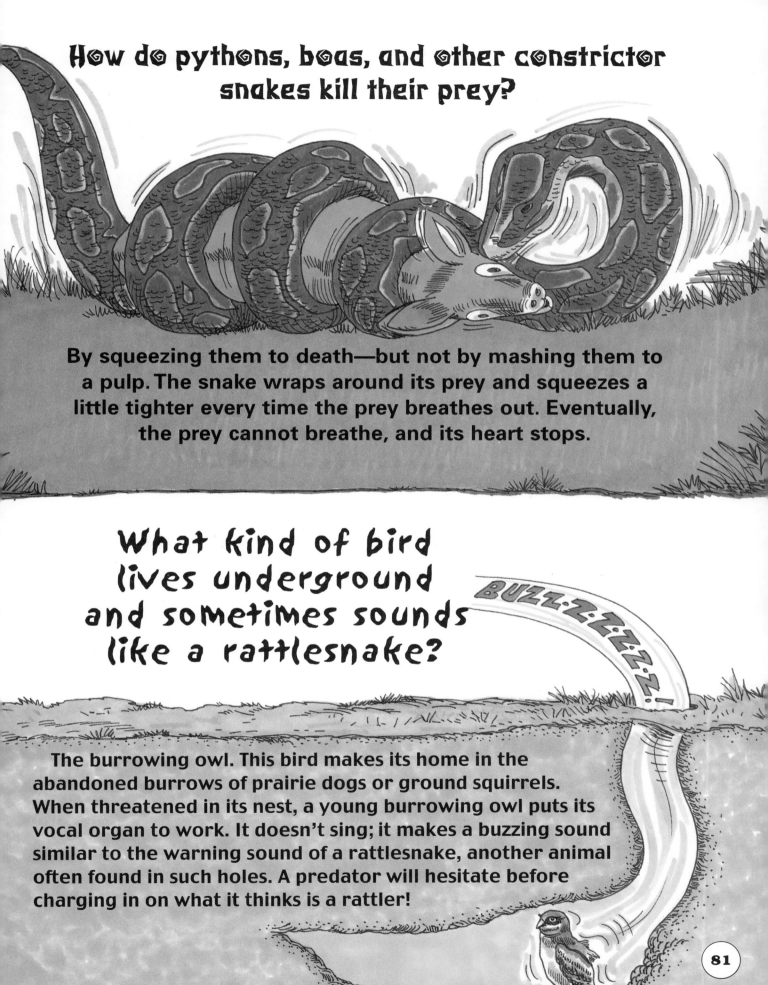

By squeezing them to death—but not by mashing them to a pulp. The snake wraps around its prey and squeezes a little tighter every time the prey breathes out. Eventually, the prey cannot breathe, and its heart stops.

What kind of bird lives underground and sometimes sounds like a rattlesnake?

BUZZ-Z-ZZ-Z!

The burrowing owl. This bird makes its home in the abandoned burrows of prairie dogs or ground squirrels. When threatened in its nest, a young burrowing owl puts its vocal organ to work. It doesn't sing; it makes a buzzing sound similar to the warning sound of a rattlesnake, another animal often found in such holes. A predator will hesitate before charging in on what it thinks is a rattler!

Why don't cuckoos build nests?

MAMA?

They don't need to. Cuckoos lay their eggs in the nests of other birds. A female cuckoo removes one of the nest owner's eggs, lays her own in its place, then leaves. The unsuspecting foster mother sits on it and, when it hatches, raises the baby cuckoo as its own.

DON'T FORGET ME ON MOTHER'S DAY!

Where do Suriname toads incubate their eggs?

In the female toad's back. The male fertilizes the eggs, then presses them into the female's back. Her skin covers the eggs until, after about 80 days, she sheds her skin. The tiny toads are set free into the water.

DON'T FORGET ME ON FATHER'S DAY—**OR** ON MOTHER'S DAY!

What makes male sea horses unusual fathers?

They give birth—sort of. The female sea horse lays her eggs into a pouch on the male's stomach. He carries the eggs and, after they hatch, carries the young for about two weeks. Then, by contracting his pouch, the male pushes out a bunch of young sea horses.

Is there a reason why baby animals look so cute?

Scientists think that the big eyes of many baby animals let adult animals know that the youngsters are harmless and need care. Some baby animals have special markings, making adult animals less likely to chase them away, as they would if adult animals entered the same territory.

How do male silk moths find their mates?

I'M HERE, DEAR!

By smell, and very well, too. The female silk moth gives off a tiny, tiny amount of scent. Experiments show that just one molecule of this substance is enough to alert a male moth to her presence. He can find her from more than a mile away!

Why do eels travel to the Sargasso Sea?

NORTH AMERICA

Sargasso Sea

WEST INDIES

SOUTH AMERICA

North Atlantic Ocean

THANKS FOR THE MAP. I'M ON MY WAY!

To **spawn** (lay eggs). The Sargasso Sea is an oval-shaped area in the North Atlantic. European freshwater eels, using their sense of smell to guide them, travel thousands of miles across the sea back to the stretch of ocean where they were born in order to lay their own eggs.

Why do birds sing?

To send other birds a message. Males do most of the singing. "This is my territory" seems to be the most common message. It may sound like a sweet song to us, but to other birds, it sounds like, "Keep out!"

For what animal were the Canary Islands named?

North Atlantic Ocean

AFRICA

CANARY ISLANDS

Dogs! The Latin word for dog is *canis*. Early explorers called the islands Canaria after the big, ferocious wild dogs they found living there. Canary birds, also found there, were named after the islands—not the other way around.

WHY ARE VULTURES GOOD TO HAVE AROUND?

Vultures are nature's clean-up crew. Experts believe that vultures living in Africa eat more meat than all the other predators combined. Without them, rotting animal carcasses would spread disease, not to mention really stink things up!

What is the only kind of bird that can fly upside down?

The hummingbird—but not for long periods of time. Little hummers also fly backwards to pull their beaks from flowers. Like helicopters, they fly up and down, hover, or zip away at more than 60 miles an hour. To do all this, their wings flap 50 to 75 times a second!

Do all tigers live in warm jungles?

No. The Siberian tiger, largest of all cats, lives in the Amur-Ussuri region of Siberia, Russia—not to mention northern China and Korea—which is covered with snow much of the year. To survive winter, the tiger grows an extra layer of fat, and its fur turns white to blend with snow.

How did guinea pigs get their name?

They were probably originally called Guiana (gee-AH-nuh) pigs because they make noises and movements that are a bit like those of regular pigs, and because Dutch traders found them in Dutch Guiana (now the independent country of Suriname), which is on South America's Caribbean coast. The animals' name eventually evolved into guinea pig.

Ducks are heavier than water, so why don't they sink?

Air trapped in ducks' feathers and held in their lungs makes them light enough to float. When a duck wants to dive under water for food, it exhales some air from its lungs to make it easier to sink. Waterproof feathers may also help ducks float.

Why do houseflies walk on food?

To find out what it tastes like. Houseflies have taste buds on their feet. If they like what they taste, they sponge saliva on the food until it dissolves, because flies can consume only liquids. Then they slurp it up!

Is there an obvious difference between centipedes and millipedes?

Centipede   Millipede

Yes, if you look closely. Centipedes have only one pair of legs on each body segment, except the last one. They can have as many as 170 segments, but the number varies; they have from 15 to 170 pairs of legs. Millipedes, on the other hand, have two pairs of legs per body segment, except for the first four. They have about 100 pairs of legs, but the actual number depends on each insect's size.

Another difference is their diet: Centipedes eat other insects, while millipedes eat only plants.

Where and why do some people celebrate Buzzard Day?

In Hinckley, Ohio, the first Sunday after March 15 is Buzzard Day. Buzzard Day celebrates the return of migrating buzzards—actually, turkey vultures—that spend each summer near Hinckley. The first birds usually reach the area about March 15 each year.

IF YOU KISS ME, I WON'T TURN INTO A PRINCE!

Are Komodo dragons the kind of dragons found in fairy tales?

No. Komodo dragons are giant lizards that live on Komodo Island and a few other islands in Indonesia, in Asia. Komodo dragons can weigh up to 300 pounds and grow as long as 10 feet. They are so big that they can eat a wild goat whole! A Komodo dragon can live to be about 100 years old.

Why might you call the hognose snake and the opossum "animal actors"?

I'M PLAYING "DEAD."

When attacked, they often play dead, because most predators are likely to lose interest in unmoving prey and leave. The opossum lies on its side, usually refusing to move even if poked or prodded. The hognose snake rolls onto its back and lets its tongue fall out of its mouth. When the coast is clear, each "actor" wakes up and dashes off.

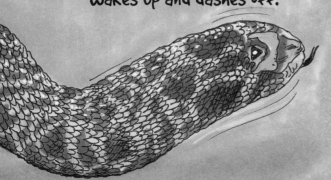

What makes the platypus an unusual mammal?

It lays eggs. Most mammals give birth to live young, except for monotremes. Monotremes are a rare group of animals with only three members: the platypus and two kinds of echidna (ih-KID-nuh), also called the spiny anteater. These animals are the only egg-laying mammals. (To make matters stranger, the platypus is also the only mammal with a duckbilled mouth.) Once eggs hatch, a monotreme mother provides her babies with milk, as other mammals do, but she doesn't have nipples. The babies suckle the milk as it oozes from her skin!

I WISH I HAD A PIZZA!

What is remarkable about the eyes of a giant squid?

Their size. Each eye measures 16 inches across—the size of an extra-large pizza! They are the biggest eyes in the world. But no one knows how well they can see.

DO OWLS NEED BRIGHT MOONLIGHT TO CATCH THEIR PREY?

No. In fact, barn owls can catch their prey in complete darkness, using their acute sense of hearing alone. Great gray owls can zero in on the sound of mice moving about in tunnels under the snow!

What strange thing happens to one eye of a baby flounder?

At first, a baby flounder has one eye on each side of its head, like every other fish. But as a flounder grows, one eye gradually moves across its head to the other side of its face. Eventually, both eyes are on the same side! The flounder spends its adult life lying on the ocean floor, eye side up.

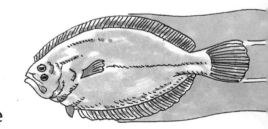

What does the four-eyed fish do with all those eyes?

I SEE YOU!

SO DO I!

It really has only two eyes, but each eye is divided into two parts. The fish lies just below the water's surface—half of each eye above water, half below. It hunts for food below, and keeps watch above for fish-eating seabirds. The four-eyed fish is also known as the anableps.

Why does a rabbit wiggle its nose?

I SMELL A CARROT!

To get a whiff of what is around it. Nose wiggling brings in air from many directions, enabling a rabbit to smell if any predators are around—or, if it is a pet rabbit, if its owner is carrying any carrots.

What kind of animals have their skeletons on the outside?

I'M THE MILLIPEDE.

I'M A BEETLE.

I'M A SPIDER.

I'M CRABBY!

Arthropods. This huge group includes insects, **arachnids** (spiders and scorpions), **crustaceans** (crabs, lobsters, and shrimps), and **myriapods** (centipedes and millipedes). Instead of having bones inside, arthropods have a hard outer surface called an exoskeleton. This shell supports and protects their squishy insides.

I'M THE CENTIPEDE.

Why don't birds fall off their perches when they sleep?

DO NOT DISTURB.

Leg locks. A bird bends its legs to perch. Bending the legs automatically pulls on muscles that make the bird's toes contract around its perch, holding the bird in place.

Why does a baby kangaroo depend on its mother's pouch?

A baby kangaroo, called a joey, is blind and helpless at birth, and weighs only a little more than a thumbtack. The joey crawls to its mother's pouch, where it finds warmth and food. It does not leave the pouch for about six months.

WOULD YOU LIKE TO HOP-ALONG WITH US?

What is an antlion?

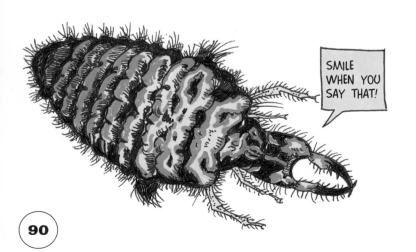

SMILE WHEN YOU SAY THAT!

The larva of a dragonfly-like insect, also known as a doodlebug. The antlion digs a cone-shaped pit into loose soil or sand, then hides at the bottom and waits for small insects to fall into the pit. While the insects struggle to climb up the steep, slippery sides of the pit to escape, the antlion snaps them up in its big jaws.

What are the hyrax's closest relatives?

*You would never guess it by looking at one, but the hyrax is related to elephants and **dugongs** (manatee-like sea mammals). The hyrax is a furry, rodentlike animal about the size of a rabbit. Hyraxes live in Africa and the Middle East.*

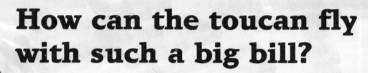

WANNA RACE?

How can the toucan fly with such a big bill?

The toucan's bill is large, but it is filled with air pockets, so it doesn't weigh much. Bright colors help the birds blend in among bright jungle colors. Thanks to its huge bill, a toucan can stand securely on a strong branch, reach for a piece of fruit, tilt its head, and gobble up its snack whole!

Which is smaller, a motmot or a mola-mola?

Definitely a motmot. The motmot is a long-tailed bird found in the forests of Central and South America. The largest are only about 20 inches long. The mola-mola, also called the ocean sunfish, is much larger. It can weigh 4,000 pounds and be 11 feet long!

Motmot

Mola-mola

Index

How many kinds of insects are there? • **Who was Jacques Cousteau?** • Why are fish slimy? •

What do spitting spiders spit? • How do diamonds form? • What is a rainbow? •

How cold does it get in Antarctica? • **Why do stars twinkle?** • What do bats eat? •

Do flying fish and flying squirrels really fly? • Is Saturn the only planet with rings? •